No Longer I Who Live

Reclaiming My Identity –
The True Story of Selina Brown

Selina Brown
with Ralph Turner

malcolm down
PUBLISHING

Copyright © 2025 Selina Brown
First published 2025 by Malcolm Down Publishing Ltd.
www.malcolmdown.co.uk

28 27 26 25   7 6 5 4 3 2 1

The right of Selina Brown to be identified as the author of this work has been asserted by her in accordance with the Copyright, Designs and Patents Act 1988.

All rights reserved. No part of this publication may be reproduced, stored in a retrieval system, or transmitted in any other form or by any means, electronic, mechanical, photocopying, recording or otherwise, without the prior permission of the publisher.

British Library Cataloguing in Publication Data
A catalogue record for this book is available from the British Library.

ISBN 978-1-915046-79-6

Scripture quotations are from The ESV® Bible (The Holy Bible, English Standard Version®), copyright © 2001 by Crossway, a publishing ministry of Good News Publishers. Used by permission. All rights reserved.

AI programmes were not used in writing this book.

Some names have been changed to protect identities.

WARNING: Some events recorded in the book relate to abuse, drugs, violence and attempted suicide and may be considered unsuitable for some readers.

Contributing writer: Ralph Turner
www.ralphturnerwriter.com

Cover concept by Selina Brown, Melanie Milongo and Richard Blaikie
Cover design by Esther Kotecha
Art direction by Sarah Grace
Back cover photograph by Mark Theisinger

Printed in the UK

Endorsements

I pray that as you read this book, hope starts rising in your heart just as it did in mine.

The strength, resilience, and determination that the woman I love has shown for so many years is extraordinary. My emotions and mind raced as I watched her push through the seemingly endless struggles and constant disappointments she faced, often bringing me to tears.

But God! Then came the moment of surrender—the Lord's voice was quiet but loving: 'You belong to Me now.' It changed Selina's life and eternity forever.

Ephesians 1:7 says, 'In him we have redemption through his blood, the forgiveness of our trespasses, according to the riches of his grace.' Amen.

Selina's life story has brought this scripture to life for me, and it is now a truth that will be forever seared on my heart.

I feel extremely proud and humbled by what she has accomplished in such a short period of time. Her passion and zeal for life are visible for everyone to see.

I look forward to the future with hope in my heart, fully persuaded that our God will accomplish more through Selina than she could ever think or imagine ... in Him.

Selina, I love you always.

Andrew Brown
Selina's husband, Co-Founder of Reboot Ministry and Pastor of Keystone Church, Walsall, UK

I dare you – read chapter one of Selina Brown's story and I promise, you will not put this book down. Not just because it's a gripping tale of sin and redemption; but because Selina makes you care about her journey even as she plunges from one self-destructive choice to another, tumbling finally to the very end of herself. You will be shocked, angry and appalled as you read; but through it all you will care, because she begins by taking you inside of her tender heart as an adopted child, desperate to know and feel that she really belongs in this world. Selina eloquently paints her thoughts and feelings as her desperate search leads inevitably to a full encounter with her heavenly Father, and her adoption into a shining new life in Christ. This book inspired and thrilled me with the bondage-breaking power of the Holy Spirit and left me with a host of deeper insights into the heart and mind of an adopted child.

Stephen Bransford
Author, You've Got a Story, The Last Photograph, Markers and Milestones. stephenbransford.com

The story of Selina Brown is a powerful testimony to the life-transforming grace of God. What began in seeming abandonment, and spiralled into a world of turmoil, addiction, and broken relationships, becomes – through the relentless love of God – a radiant display of redemption and hope. Page after page, God's grace shines with ever-increasing brilliance, proving that no heart is too far and no life too broken for His healing touch.

This book is a must-read for anyone who feels they are beyond God's reach – outside His love, His kingdom, or His purpose. It will inspire faith, stir hope, and reveal the deep compassion of our Saviour.

Selina and Andrew Brown are dear friends and a Spirit-filled couple whose lives radiate the love of Christ. Knowing where they came from only magnifies what God has done – and it's nothing short of miraculous.

Pastor Rick McFarland
River Rock Church, Colorado Springs, Colorado, USA

Wow! *No Longer I Who Live* is a phenomenal story and told so well! I found it hard to put down!

Riveting from the start and often extremely painful as she bears all, I greatly rejoiced with tears when I finally read of Selina's true salvation after a very damaged, dark and debased life. And a full-on miracle that she stayed alive long enough to receive Jesus, being fought at every turn by the enemy to try and keep it from happening. Praise God, he lost!

This story has helped open my own eyes, to have more compassion towards hurting, hardened people. So many have tough outer shells, flaunting a façade to try and protect their own deceived and wounded hearts and broken souls, whose lives have been all but destroyed by Satan. I pray this book and this story will make its way into the hands of countless millions who need to know the only Living God, their true Heavenly Father, and experience His transformational love through receiving Jesus.

Jill LeBlanc
Published songwriter and recording artist, alongside husband Charlie LeBlanc

I remember the day I met Selina. I was drawn to her. It was my first visit to Charis Bible College and her first year there. This was a woman with a story. Her face and body were still marked by the scars of pain, addiction, and brokenness, but I could see God's restoration and healing in her. When I returned a year later, the radiance of Christ had given her a different look. The look of Christ in Selina is what she carries more of, year after year.

Paul writes, 'I have been crucified with Christ. It is no longer I who live, but Christ who lives in me.' This book is a declaration of God's relentless grace and the freedom found only in Christ. Only Jesus can write Selina's story. I love you, Selina; I love knowing you, and I love the fact *No Longer I Who Live* testifies that God can make all things new. Selina's life may look like a miracle, but this book proves that God wants to write the miracle into all our lives. May this beautiful book be used for that purpose.

Andrea Williams
Chief Executive, Christian Legal Centre and Christian Concern

I am excited to recommend this amazing story of amazing grace! Selina shares the painful, raw reality of living with a stolen identity of how her past tried to define her and hold her captive, but as she eventually finds her new identity in Christ, the transformation is definitely supernatural. The story is riveting, and you won't want to put the book down once you start reading it. It's incredible how she was able to reclaim her identity.

I remember the first time I met her. As part of the faculty at Charis Bible College in Colorado, I was ministering at the Charis location in Walsall, England and I knew by the Spirit that God had His hand on her life from the moment that I met her. I had the privilege of ministering to her, and it's been amazing to see how from the moment Selina gave God her 'yes' how God has blessed her and is now using her to touch nations. She is such a trophy of grace, and her story is again a testimony that God can take any mess and turn it into a message that will in turn help so many people realise that the abundant life so many are searching for, is only found in Christ.

To see how God is using Selina and Andrew in ministry now and the restoration of their family is truly a miracle that only God could have done! The person that Selina was is dead and gone, and truly out of her dying to her old life, she found a new identity in Christ and now she is living her new life in Christ.

Daniel Amstutz
Director of Healing Ministry at Charis Bible College, Colorado, and president of Daniel Amstutz Collective, Inc.

What a remarkable testimony of a life transformed by the amazing grace of God! Desperately searching for love throughout a lifetime of struggles and heartache, Selina was wonderfully drawn by the perfect love of God. Finding her identity in Christ caused her heart to be completely healed and restored and changed for eternity. Her story reflects His story – He came to save that which was lost – Selina's life redeemed by His amazing love, mercy and grace!

Susan Donnelly
Former Pastor, Glen Aros Church, Dumfries, Scotland
susan@jsdonnelly.co.uk

A lady once told me, 'I was so low, that when I reached up, I couldn't touch the bottom!' What a place to be; utter hopelessness and despair.

Romans 15:13 reads, 'May the God of hope fill you with all joy and peace in believing, so that by the power of the Holy Spirit you may abound in hope.' Paul begins the verse with the words, 'May the God of hope fill you.' This is a wonderful reminder that God is the source of our hope. In a world filled with hopelessness and despair, Paul prays that believers will continue to draw from a well of hope that will never run dry. After all, God is both the source and the sustainer of our hope. Paul's description of God as the 'God of hope' signifies that, even when the future seems uncertain and unpredictable, God's steadfast love and faithfulness will keep our minds in perfect peace (Isaiah 26:3).

As you read this book you will discover what our dear friend Selina found, that even in your darkest moment, in your battle against despair, there is still hope.

Selina's life was saved, was rescued by the love, grace and mercy of God. From being at the point of taking her own life, she turned to the God of hope, to Jesus, and her life was never the same again. In Romans 15:13, Paul prays that the God of hope would fill us with 'all joy and peace.' Here, we see that hope is connected to the qualities of joy and peace. In other words, hope generates joy and peace within us, even in the face of adversity.

Romans 15:13 is a heartfelt prayer and blessing for believers to experience the fullness of God's hope, joy, and peace 'by the power of the Holy Spirit.' When faced with moments of uncertainty, we must continue to depend on the power of the Holy Spirit, for without Him we can do nothing. This is how Selina now leads her life, continuing to depend upon the Holy Spirit. Her life has been transformed by the love of God, and so can yours.

John Donnelly
Former Pastor, Glen Aros Church, Dumfries, Scotland
john@jsdonnelly.co.uk

I first met Selina when she came for her interview at Charis Bible College in Walsall, UK. From that very moment, I sensed a powerful calling on her life – I even said, 'You're going to be an evangelist.' The love of Christ was evident in her eyes, radiating with purpose and hope.

Reading *No Longer I Who Live* has only deepened my respect for Selina's journey. This book is a raw, honest, and deeply moving account of a life transformed by God's grace, love and mercy. Selina shares her pain and hardships with a vulnerability that is both heart-wrenching and faith-building. Her story is a vivid reminder that no brokenness is beyond the reach of God's redemptive power.

Every page reflects the mercy and unrelenting love of Christ – how He restores, redefines, and gives purpose. Selina's testimony is not just inspiring – it's a clear witness to the healing and identity we find in Him.

I wholeheartedly recommend this book to anyone seeking encouragement, healing, or a deeper understanding of their true identity in Christ. It will stir your faith and remind you of the life-transformative power of the Gospel.

Ken Chang
Founder, Chang Ministries Global

Gripping from beginning to the end, lives transformed, healed and set free only Jesus could accomplish this and how He has. To the reader, this is the reality of Christ in us! Enjoy every word –it's truth.

Will Graham
Kingdom Highways – Ministry of Will & Barbara Graham

It is my privilege and honour to endorse Selina's book to you… I never knew Selina before she was saved and transformed by Jesus… and to be honest, if she didn't share her testimony with you in spoken or written word, you would never know… this lady is a new creation in Christ, a living testimony of the grace of God, not only transformed by Jesus herself, but now together with her husband Andrew (who also has a powerful testimony!) they are leading thousands to Jesus all over the world through their 'Reboot' ministry and making an impact in Walsall UK through the wonderful Keystone church they have planted there to serve their community with the love of God, and the power of The Gospel. From rejection to love, addiction to freedom, hopelessness to hope, and death to life, this book, Selina's life story, is a powerful testimony to the amazing, saving, and transforming grace of God!

Jonathan Conrathe
Founder and Director, Mission24

Captivating and deeply moving. Having been a close friend of Selina's for nine years, I thought I knew her story – yet this autobiography reveals a depth of trauma and heartbreak no one should ever have to endure. What makes her journey so extraordinary isn't just the pain she survived, but the profound transformation she experienced after encountering her Saviour.

The change in Selina's life is nothing short of miraculous. The girl who once preferred solitude has become a vibrant, magnetic presence – someone who naturally draws people in with warmth, authenticity, and joy. Selina is now a community builder, a trusted friend to many, and a beacon of hope.

This book is impossible to put down. It's a powerful testimony of how God redeems brokenness and brings beauty from ashes. What the enemy intended for harm, God is using for an abundant harvest. Selina ministers with a depth, passion, and sensitivity that could only come from walking through the fire and choosing to let God refine her in it. She is a strong woman of God – secure in her identity, unwavering in her faith, and deeply aware of who she belongs to.

Her story will inspire, challenge, and bless you.

Alison Beechey
Receptionist/Purchasing Assistant, Andrew Wommack
Ministries, Europe

Selina's story is one of extremes. From the pit of hopelessness and despair to the joy of a life totally surrendered to God, Selina's dramatic transformation vividly expresses the truth that 'where sin increased, grace abounded all the more' (Romans 5:20). Every chapter compelling, down to earth and candid, this book is evidence that God's love, liberating power and His gift of a unique and fulfilling purpose are ready and waiting to be experienced by whosoever would like to discover them, no matter where they have come from.

Lucy Curtis-Prior
Dean of Students, Charis Bible College, Walsall

Blessings Galore to you all who will read this book. Discovering the importance of people in the pursuit of greatness is one of the best ways we can make it in life. It is important to be aware that from cradle to eternal life, we will always have people pave our way, but God, in the Lordship of Jesus, will help us succeed and fulfil our destiny. You will see Jesus through a lens of love and also see yourself as a leader, no matter where you are. Selina and Andrew realise that, through the vulnerability of telling the truth to us all as we read.

Shirley Mifetu
Finance Assistant, Andrew Wommack Ministries, Europe

To Jesus, the Lover of my soul who gave His life for me, and to my grandson Kaiden, now safe in His arms until we meet again.

Contents

Foreword	17
Introduction	21
1. When Did You Find Me?	23
2. Letters to God	35
3. Walk Behind Me	45
4. One Too Many	55
5. Six Children by Twenty	61
6. The Stalker	69
7. Cuckoo in the Nest	77
8. Discovering the Past	89
9. The Scrounger Shame of the Baby Machine	99
10. Breaking Point	107
11. The Vodka and the Knife	117
12. Random Facebook	129
13. Darkness to Light	137
14. Identity Change	147
15. The Drummer with the Smile	155
16. Reboot	163
17. Family	173
18. Keystone	181
19. …But Christ Who Lives	189
A Letter from Selina	195
A Gospel Picture	197
Acknowledgements	199
About	201

Foreword

I'm very honoured to write this foreword to Selina's book, *No Longer I Who Live*. In Selina's case, that title accurately describes the life she now lives. She has truly exchanged her broken life for the supernatural life that Jesus is living through her. Selina is a trophy of God's grace and a wonderful testimony to His relentless pursuit of us no matter who we are or what we've done.

I first encountered Selina when she came to our Grace and Faith Conference in Telford, England in 2016. She was among hundreds of people who came forward in that meeting and she received Jesus as her personal Saviour and the baptism of the Holy Spirit. Even though there were hundreds of people who came to the front, I remember seeing Selina transformed right before my eyes. She stood out. You could see that she was experiencing the Lord in a powerful way.

I didn't have personal contact with her until later as I ministered at our Charis Bible College in Walsall, England, where she became a student. I got a brief, two-minute version of her testimony then and, over the years, I've learnt more and watched her grow into a mature believer who has not only been changed but is being mightily used by the Lord to reach out and to change others.

However, it was only as I read this book that I realised the depths that she descended into before finally finding her life in Jesus. This is a powerful read that will hold your attention to the very end. That's certainly the way it was with me.

Selina went through more traumatic experiences than most of us will ever encounter. Although Selina doesn't make excuses for what she did, she does give insight into what was going on inside of her that will not only bless those who know the saving power of Jesus, but that is a powerful witness to anyone who is still searching and looking for love and acceptance in all the wrong places. Selina makes it crystal clear that Jesus is the only answer to all life throws at us.

Selina's testimony shouts to me that the Lord loves us unconditionally. He isn't waiting on us to clean up our act before He helps us. If we could get free on our own, we wouldn't need Him. Rather, Jesus is waiting for us to come to the end of ourselves where we can let Him take control.

This is what Selina did and the goodness of the Lord in her life now is a testimony to all of us that the Lord's plans for us are good (Jer. 29:11). Selina found her husband Andrew Brown and together, they are taking the same truths that set them free to others all over the world. The Lord redeemed all the suffering Selina went through and is using it to give hope to the hopeless.

You will be blessed beyond measure to see how this prodigal daughter reunited with her Heavenly Father. Selina's story shows that you can't go beyond His reach. Regardless of where you are or how deep the pit you find yourself in, God's power to save is as close as your cry for help.

Thank you, Selina, for candidly sharing all you've been through so others can come to know the same love, joy and purpose you've experienced. The best is still ahead for you and Andrew. Only eternity will reveal the full extent of the great things He is doing through you.

Andrew Wommack
Andrew Wommack Ministries

Introduction

The crash was deafening. A metal-twisting, glass-shattering moment. And then—silence. A hollow, suffocating silence.

I was still alive.

A wave of despair hit me harder than the impact itself. This wasn't supposed to happen. I wasn't supposed to be alive.

Pathetic. I couldn't even get this right.

Half a bottle of Smirnoff burning in my veins, I had climbed behind the wheel, determined that today would be my last. The motorway bridge was waiting. One sharp turn, one final moment, and it would all be over.

But instead, here I was, broken, bleeding. But breathing. My head had smashed through the windscreen, my legs tangled in the wreckage of the dashboard. Fifty miles an hour. No seatbelt. And yet, against all odds, I had survived.

Was this some kind of cruel joke? Or was there a God after all?

That question had haunted me for years. It followed me through every high and low, whispering in the quiet moments, shouting into the craziness, demanding an answer. I searched for it in all the wrong places, I ran from it, I fought it—until. Until that day.

Chapter One

When Did You Find Me?

The gas fire was warm, spluttering away in the corner. I curled up on the sofa, pulling my feet under me. Wrapping my dressing gown around me, I snuggled into Mum's side.

'Mum... When was it? When was it that you found me? Why did you find me? Tell me the story.'

I was five years old, and it wasn't the first time I'd asked. It was a comforting story to hear. Me being rescued from an adoption agency, finding a new mum and dad, finding a brand-new life.

Even as a five-year-old, I was aware that there were things I didn't know. Things I wanted to know. Things that made me feel uneasy. Had I been abandoned? Why was I abandoned? Who was my real mum? Why had she left me?

Lying against my adopted mum's side that weekday evening, there were more questions than answers. But at the same time, such an awareness, such a comfort, an assurance that I was loved.

'Selina, you've heard that story so many times! You know how it was. We couldn't have children, and we had adopted Anthony. We so wanted him to have a sister. And that was you!'

'Tell me what the nuns said!'

'Sweetheart, you know! When we were brought into the adoption agency, the nuns told us you were the ugliest baby they had ever seen! They said we could walk right past you if we didn't want you. But of course, you weren't in the least bit ugly. You're beautiful. We chose you.'

With a smile on my face, I snuggled closer. The comfort of knowing that even though someone else had rejected me, I had been found. I had been loved.

The Father Hudson Adoption Agency

The Father Hudson Agency doesn't always get a good press. It's one of the adoption agencies for the Catholic Church in Birmingham. Mum and Dad – my adopted mum and dad – were Catholics, so it was the obvious place to go. And that's how I ended up at our house on Wolverhampton Road, Walsall, in the West Midlands, along with Anthony, adopted two years earlier.

I'm mixed race, with a father possibly from Asia, that much I do know. Were the nuns' comments about me being ugly to do with my colour? Possibly.

My birth mum had left me at the agency. Her boyfriend had given her a choice, him or me. She chose him.

I stayed with the agency for the first three months of my life, until Mum and Dad came along.

My adoption was what is called a 'closed adoption'. It's not allowed anymore, but in those days, back in 1982, it was pretty common. In closed adoption cases, all records of my birth mother and any other information are deliberately destroyed. My birth identity ceases to exist. The idea was that I didn't have a past.

But I did. And growing up, that past was going to haunt me.

Birth Wounds

I've been alive since the moment I was conceived. For nine months, I grew inside my mother, hearing her voice, feeling her movements, knowing her presence. That was my whole world—safe, warm and familiar.

Then, suddenly, I was born. And just like that, I lost everything I knew. I was separated from her, the one person I had bonded with before I even took my first breath. Imagine the shock. The confusion. The grief.

But I was just a baby, right? Too young to understand?

That's the thing—babies feel more than we realise. And I felt it. I was passed from one temporary caregiver to another for three months before my adoptive parents took me home. Three months of unfamiliar faces, different voices, and the constant, unanswered longing for the person who had carried me. I had no words for it, but the loss was real.

People talk a lot more now about what babies experience in the womb—how they hear, feel, and even form connections. And there's a lot of research on adopted children and why so many of us struggle with deep feelings of loss, anger, and rejection, even in the most loving homes. Why we push boundaries harder, act out in ways that seem extreme, and carry a vulnerability that never fully disappears.

It's not just teenage rebellion. It's something deeper. Being adopted means carrying an invisible wound—a wound that doesn't heal with time. Mum and Dad didn't know it then, but that was to be my journey. I needed to know I was loved, to be constantly reminded of it, to be told, again and again, that story of being chosen at the adoption agency. And despite that, deep inside, there was that awareness of hurt, of rejection. Of loss. Where was my real mother? What happened to her? The bond from the womb was a constant tug at my soul. The need for something more than could ever be offered by adopted parents. It wasn't their fault of course, but as far as I was concerned, growing up, it may as well have been!

Outsider

I was one of the few dark-skinned children in the school. Definitely the only mixed-race girl. Definitely the only adopted child. Add to that a caution of opening myself up to any friend in case I got hurt, in case I was rejected, and I ended up a bit of a loner.

There were a couple of friends, Jenny and Clare. Like me, they were outsiders too. We hated dressing up in a glamorous way, we hated the girl gangs with their glitz and make-up and their passion for the pop group Take That. Clare decided she was a lesbian. That meant that she was immediately outside the friendship groups among the girls. We found ourselves sitting together at school, pretty much because no one else would.

I was actually quite bright at my studies, nearly top of the class, when I wanted to work. But the underlying insecurities of adoption were always playing into who I was.

At one moment I would be the ideal pupil, properly dressed in the school uniform, a long dark braid down my back, and being used as an illustration in assembly by the headmistress as to how to dress. And at another moment, I would be a nightmare for the form teacher, angry, petulant, abusive, sulky.

'I'm having a birthday party next Saturday. Everyone's invited. But don't tell Selina.'

The thing is, I heard it said. More than once. I pretended I didn't care, that I wasn't interested in being with that group of girls anyway. I kind of convinced myself that I really *didn't* care. But there was always that hurt on the inside.

Sometimes it was a bit brutal. Like the time we went away as a class for a couple of nights. I was ten years old at the time. Still feeling insecure, I took my teddy. Big mistake. The other girls got hold of him and gave him a fake trial—the punishment was death by hanging from the rafters.

Injuries

The neighbours called me the naughty one. I lived up to it, delighting in ringing their doorbells and running away. I'd be out, running around the estate we lived on practically every spare hour I had before it got dark. Patch, our Border Collie cross, would watch me go rather longingly! I'd be out with Jenny and Clare occasionally, but mainly it was just me.

The council estate we lived on was fairly new at the time, built in the late 1970s. Decent sized semi-detached houses for the most part. Gas fires, gas central heating, early pvc style windows, a small garden. All a bit crammed in, but there was plenty of space to explore further afield. Playing fields to the south, a smaller open area next to the primary school at the top of the road. Even a local nature reserve if I could be bothered to walk that far.

The residents for the most part were third and fourth generation working class people from the Black Country area. They could be as hard as nails, but as soft as butter if they liked you. And super protective should anyone dare to badmouth their housing estate in the press!

I was free to roam, and it was pretty safe to do so, with neighbours looking out for one another. But there was a bit of a lack of care, a lack of boundaries as a child, which got me into more than a few scrapes. Aside from the fights with the oh-so-nice girls at school, I managed to damage myself on a number of occasions. A broken nose, a broken arm. Danger was not a word I would consider. The harder the tree was to climb, the more fun it was. The harder the tackle I could put in on the football field, the better.

Mum and Dad were not exactly the best of carers in this respect. They didn't believe I had broken my arm until I pretty much forced them to take me to the hospital. One time, I got one of Mum's sewing needles embedded in my foot and it took two weeks for them to believe me and do something about it.

In a way, even the pain was welcome. It added to the hard-nosed persona I was developing. My mechanism for not being hurt, for dealing with rejection from the other girls, was to be more and more the tom-boy, more and more the hard tackler in football, the no-nonsense kid who would hit first and ask questions later.

Books

I was last to be chosen in team sports. It was deliberate on the part of the other girls as I was actually one of the best at most sports. Again, I pretended I didn't care. But inside, it was burning. Inside was a continuous raging at the world that found its way out in an occasional fight or screaming match with the girls at school. With my parents too. Pretty much anything would trigger me, and Mum and Dad were running out of ways to manage me. Better to ignore it, to pacify me, to leave me alone.

And I was alone a lot of the time. When not on the streets, I was locked in my bedroom with my books. I was an avid reader from an early age. All the Enid Blyton books I could get my hands on as I grew. *The Secret Seven*, *The Famous Five*. As I got older, the whole series of the young adult books, *Sweet Valley High* by Francine Pascal became preferred reading—over seventy of them! One of the books was called *Outcast*. I liked that one. Of course I did.

I spent as much time as I could in the local library, away from others, but also in the company of a vast army—writers, poets, thinkers, lovers, travellers and explorers. Authors that could take me away from the life I faced. That could carry me to imaginary lands, impossible adventures and wonderful relationships. I even liked the *smell* of the books! I still do it—lift a book to my nose and breathe in. There's something about the smell of an old book that takes me right back to that library.

Abandoned

Being in the football team meant practices after school. Mum and Dad were always good at collecting me afterwards. Until they weren't.

Mum thought Dad was collecting me. Dad thought Mum was collecting me. So neither showed up. It was all sorted out; I got home okay. Except that it was a trigger for some extreme behaviour.

I felt totally rejected. The emotions I experienced as I stood with the teacher after all the other kids had gone—I can still remember the feeling. Raw terror at having been abandoned. A queasiness in my stomach, a deep, deep dread.

I was frightened. So frightened. Afraid that Mum and Dad had been killed in an accident. Afraid to be alone.

I was only eight years old at this stage, and being left at school was a big thing. So much so that for the next three months, Mum not only had to take me to school personally but sit outside the classroom during the school day. It was the only way she and the teachers could get me to attend. Dad would take me out at lunchtime – against the school rules, but again, the only way I could cope with lunchtimes.

The teachers did their best.

'Selina, you are special! You were chosen! Not many children get to have that in their lives.'

The words didn't help. Being 'chosen' meant I had been 'un-chosen' by my real mother.

The freak accident of leaving me at school brought to the surface all the suppressed fears and emotions of an adopted kid. Impulsive. Provocative. Aggressive. Fearful. Antisocial. They were all there, all playing their role in creating the character of an abandoned child in my heart and mind.

The Bus Stop

My adoption issues were always there. Always bubbling along under the surface, waiting for an opportunity to appear.

Sarah lived on the same estate as me in Walsall. One day, we'd been fighting. I guess it was spite, but Sarah wrote in big letters on the glass of the bus stop outside our house, 'Selina's Mum can't have kids, that's why she's adopted'. It hurt. It really hurt. When Dad found out, he sent me upstairs out of the way. Mum was in tears that night.

I dealt with it alone. Once again in my room. Once again on my own.

I fed off the abandonment. I allowed it to become my master. To affect my moods, my behaviour, my attitudes. There were so many bust-ups with Mum and Dad. How many times did they get close to throwing me out? How many times did I nearly run away?

The words on the bus stop were ruling my whole life.

Church

Mum and Dad were Catholics of course, and that meant church on Sundays. Dad used to go to an earlier service, so it was Mum who took Anthony and me to St Joseph's in Bentley, a short drive from our housing estate.

I think I have a thing about smells. The smell of the prayer books of course. And of the incense. I can't remember much else from my childhood days at church, but the smell of the incense has stayed with me. It represented what it was meant to, I guess. The mystical, the other-worldly. A place away from the day to day. So, a place I appreciated, longed to be in.

Mum's parents came to church too and Anthony and I spent a lot of time with them in the holidays. It was fun to visit the library with them, to play in the garden, to look through the cabinets in their lounge, full of trinkets that were especially attractive to inquisitive children.

Dad's mum was not far away either. She made the best roast potatoes I've ever tasted! We enjoyed the treats from our grandparents.

Treats from Mum and Dad too. They really were trying to do their best. We'd go out for days at the seaside. Rhyl on the Welsh coast was a favourite. Parks, even theme parks, were part of holiday time. Often the neighbour's kids would come along too. Mum and Dad were forever hospitable. There were always parties for our birthdays and even if I didn't have close friends to invite, the kids from the neighbourhood were there.

With my Catholic background, I was aware that there must be a God. A God of the smells, a God of the incense, a God far away. And a God I was sure that had no love for me. How could He? He'd abandoned me at birth, and I had, as sure as anything, abandoned Him with my behaviour.

Yet I knew He was there. Maybe He did care?

It wasn't just the question I asked Mum as I curled up next to her on the sofa, it was the question I would ask God too.

'When did You find me?'

The thing is, I had no idea of the answer.

Chapter Two

Letters to God

Dear God

I'm sorry. I'm so sorry.

It's not that I mean to be like this. I know I can do better. But I just feel so angry!

I know you don't like me. I know you can't love me. How could you possibly love someone like me? With all this I've done. With all that I'm thinking. I hate myself, God, I wish I was dead.

But I will try harder. I will…

I remember writing letters to God from around the age of twelve or thirteen. My life was already out of control. At least, it felt that way. My constant awareness of having been adopted, of not knowing who my birth mother was, that feeling of unwavering rejection was always with me.

How to Live

I didn't know how to live. In fact, I wasn't sure I wanted to live. The thoughts of suicide and self-harming were never far away.

I remember some of my early songwriting efforts. This was one of the first:

> *I'm always on the outside, always looking in. Death seems the best option, but suicide's a sin.*

I was too young to understand the confessional box at the Catholic Church but, in my mind, I was forever confessing my sins. I believed in God. I knew there was a God. But the God I was talking to was so strict. A God of rules and regulations. Someone who had little time for a twisted up twelve-year-old kid intent on wrecking her life. After all, I argued, I was an adopted kid. A baby who had not been wanted, who had lost her mother, lost hope... Lost the will to live.

How was I supposed to put this all together? Did adopted kids have rules to live by? What were their reference points? How were they meant to interact with the rest of the world?

One of my teachers at school told me I was special; chosen even. But I didn't feel it. At the age of twelve, with puberty beginning, my emotions were all over the place. I was desperately looking for love, for a real reason to live. But all I saw was rejection.

> *Dear God, please take my life.*

The Youth Group

Clare the lesbian had become Clare the Christian.

'Please come Selina! Why not? Youth group's every Friday night, there's loads of kids there. It's a lot of fun. Come along!'

So I did.

It was a new style church, not a denominational one. The kind of place where you were more likely to be given a hug than a handshake. And it was genuinely a lot of fun.

I met Steph. She was a youth worker assigned to the church for a year. She listened, she understood, she prayed. I had found a friend, someone who could help.

Clare and I joined in with the games, the table tennis, even the bible studies. It felt like the youth group was really helping me. It was giving me some kind of identity, a new group of friends who were on my side. I even started going to the church services on Sunday morning. But it didn't last.

His name was Steve.

I was twelve years old. He was twenty-four.

The Vine

The church helped to run a coffee shop in the centre of Walsall called The Vine. As well as being part of the church, Steve had a job at The Vine and it wasn't long before I was calling in most evenings after school.

It was a fun place to hang out. Lots of colourful characters came through that door. The Vine attracted many of the street people, offering them a warm haven and a good cup of tea. Prostitutes as well, from the nearby red-light district. There were a lot of Asian lads there too, quietly pulling away from the religious expectations of their parents.

The music was good—they had an old-fashioned jukebox. There were pool tables to play at, and it wasn't hard to feel part of a family, even if it was a rather dysfunctional one!

'You're really lovely Selina, no one should tell you you're not wanted. I think you're beautiful.'

He was quite a bit taller than me. A white guy, dark hair. Big smile. Reaching out, he put his hand on my shoulder.

I didn't go out of my way to look good. There was no lipstick or makeup. My hair was long and dark, tied back in a ponytail. I wore T-shirts and baggy jogging bottoms. Nothing to look at really. So, I was genuinely flattered. And this wasn't just one of the boys at school, this was Steve, a twenty-four-year-old man. He was paying attention to me. To me! He'd buy me drinks, sit down with me and chat when he had the chance. I liked his company.

'What are you doing on Saturday morning? Fancy a walk around the park?'

And so it began. Kisses and cuddles at first. Just being together—shopping, coffee. Text messages every day. I took him over to the house and Mum and Dad seemed to like him. Like any impressionable girl, I was rather pleased to have hooked such a significant catch. That was definitely one-up on the glamour girls at school. The rumours got around that I was dating a twenty-four-year-old. I was quietly pleased they did.

Questions

I was twelve. He was twenty-four. There were bound to be questions.

Emma and Malcolm, the youth group leaders, appeared at the house one day to talk to Mum and Dad. They explained what they thought was happening and that as a result, Steve was no longer a part of the church, nor able to work at The Vine.

Nowadays, an exclusion from church activities would be seen as a light punishment. There should have been a report to the police, safeguarding policies to be followed, and more. But back in the day, that was as serious as it got. So, Steve and I were simply able to ignore it.

Mum and Dad asked a few questions but accepted what was happening. Dad seemed even to facilitate it, suggesting we go up to my bedroom when Steve visited, rather than stay in the lounge with them.

It wasn't just my mum and dad. Steve's parents were leaders in another church and sure enough, on visiting them, they also allowed us to go upstairs to Steve's bedroom. Steve had moved back home soon after we started dating. I helped him pack up, finding along the way, a set of hardcore pornographic magazines. It pointed me in the direction I would take. With a bit of wisdom, I'd have walked away from that relationship, but it was all too late.

What started as kissing and petting got more serious. I lost my virginity aged twelve.

Why did my dad facilitate the relationship? Did he not care? Did he really think it was okay for me to date Steve? Maybe he just wanted an easy life. He would have been aware of my possible reaction should he have tried to stop it. Perhaps he felt that it was a way of keeping me in check—and in sight.

Out of Sight

I wasn't really in sight though. When I wasn't dating Steve, I was at The Vine still or just walking around Walsall at night. I found a few like-minded kids. Broken, harmed, abused, hurting—and doing practically anything to stay away from their dysfunctional home lives. Clare was one of them, of course. Then there was Pete, Adam and Craig.

What we did, didn't end well for those three boys. Today, Pete is an alcoholic. Adam died of a heart attack, brought on by his lifestyle. I lost touch with Craig and have no idea what happened to him. Craig, if ever you get to read these words, get in touch. I want you to know that God is real, that He's not just a story from a book and that He loves you. He really does, just the way you are.

Not that I knew that myself in those days.

The five of us would stroll around the streets. Clare would usually go home after a while, leaving the four of us to spend the whole of the night walking the streets, getting into trouble. The police got to know us, with the usual greeting of 'Do your parents know you're out?' Occasionally they drove us home. Mum and Dad reported me missing the first few times I stayed out, and the police would find me and take me home on those occasions. But once Mum and Dad stopped reporting me, the police didn't really bother us much unless we were being violent or abusive. For the most part, we sat on corners, drinking and smoking. We weren't above stealing either. One night we took a whole barrel of beer from outside a pub and hid it away. It lasted a week.

Alcohol and cigarettes came early for me. The gang of us would pool our resources and ask an adult to go into the off-licence to buy us drinks. Super strength Skol lager and an alcopop called MD 20/20 were the favourites. 20/20 was a particularly strong alcopop, advertised as 20% alcohol in 20-ounce bottles. Or to put it another way, a standard 750ml bottle of MD 20/20 contains 10.5 units of alcohol. A regular 275ml alcopop has just 1.5 units. 20/20 was a quicker way to get drunk.

I hadn't bothered with smoking at first, but on one particular night, I was so drunk, I decided to smoke a whole pack of Benson & Hedges. That's when it began: I was hooked on smoking, aged thirteen.

Drugs

And it wasn't just smoking cigarettes. Cannabis followed. Clare would have nothing to do with this but along with Pete, Adam and Craig, the four of us could be found hidden away in back streets, late at night, passing around a joint.

Walsall had its own drug drive through. All you had to do was lower the window, hand over a £20 note and a packet of good quality cannabis was all yours.

It was Dad who first found out I was smoking cannabis.

'I can smell it on you! You can't try and fool me on this one, Selina!'

The thing is, the next thing I know is him giving me a £20 note and driving me over to drug alley to buy it. He was facilitating my relationship with Steve and now he was buying me drugs and taking me over there to get them. His way of controlling a young teenager who was otherwise completely out of control.

Out of Control

My letters to God, whether literal or in my head, were becoming more and more frequent. I felt so condemned. I knew what I was doing was not what God would want. Increasingly being off my head. Sex with Steve, and with other men too. Staying out all night, skipping off school the next day. Shouting at my mum and dad all the time. Angry. I was so angry.

And then, those letters. The cry of a lost kid to a Father in Heaven. But still, at this stage, a Father who would condemn me as much as I condemned myself.

> *Dear God, please forgive me. I know I keep doing bad things. I know what I'm doing is wrong and I know you must hate me for it, but I don't know how to stop.*

How could God ever love me? I was deep into drink and drugs, smoking all the time and carrying on an affair with a twenty-four-year-old man. Things really were out of control.

I decided that if God didn't love me, and if no one else seemed to care, maybe it was best just to take my own life.

It started with self-harming. I would steal my dad's razor and cut my arms. In a way, the pain felt good. After all, to my twisted mind, this is what I deserved. I would rub my school ruler up and down on my arms vigorously, to and fro, to and fro, until there were burn marks. I'd wear long sleeves at school but got caught out one time in Physical Education class. My parents were called in and asked whether they knew about it.

It got worse. Cigarette burns, cutting my hands with glass. I was so angry. Angry at life. And angry with myself. I wasn't really blaming others—but I did blame myself. A kid still aged thirteen. Into drink and drugs. Having sex with an adult. It must be my fault, it must be... So, the pain was the punishment.

When my friends at school questioned me, I blamed the dog for the cuts and bruises.

I just didn't care. I really didn't care! On the basis that no one loved me, why should I? I drank more, smoked more cigarettes, smoked more cannabis. It wasn't as if my parents were great drinkers, but they had a cupboard full of various spirits. One time I drank so much from their drinks cabinet that I wet myself.

My downward turn had been noticed at The Vine. I was more often outside getting drunk than inside playing pool. Some of the Asian lads were genuinely concerned.

'Selina, why are you doing this? What's it about? Please stop!'

That was Hasan. At seventeen, he was one of the leaders amongst the Asian boys. He began to look out for me. On more than one occasion he picked me up off the streets and drove me home. On at least one occasion, he even cleaned the vomit off my clothes.

It was Dad who found me one night. He actually kicked in the bedroom door to get to me. I was lying on the floor with empty pill bottles surrounding me. Earlier, I had called in at the petrol station across the road and bought as many pain relief tablets as I could. I swallowed them with the help of the contents of a vodka bottle. Added to that, I took my dad's prescription tablets. I had no idea what they were for.

Dad got me to hospital in time.

It was as I was recovering from this particular episode that I wrote the beginning of a new song:

Once I let you close to me, but then I let you go ...
Dear God, where are you now?

Chapter Three

Walk Behind Me

Hasan was concerned. He saw what was happening. As my relationship with Steve developed, it became more and more unhealthy. Steve became controlling, telling me what to do, where to go. Stopping me meeting up with friends.

I decided to get away from him. Clare and I got particularly drunk one Sunday and, in the spur of the moment, decided to take the train to Leicester. Leicester was where our church friend Steph now lived. Maybe she could help with the bullying I was receiving from Steve? A drunken decision, but Steph could genuinely help us.

Leicester

Actually, we were more than a bit drunk. We'd filled a coke bottle with most of the contents of my parents' drinks cupboard—whisky, rum, vodka, all mixed together. Disguised in colour with a bit of coke. We had enough money to get to Birmingham station but no further. Standing outside the station, we begged for money. In the end, a lady believed our made-up story of needing to get 'home to Leicester' and gave us the money we needed.

I had Steph's address but, of course, we hadn't called her in advance. We stood on the pavement for a while, but it was clear there was no one in. What to do now? I had no wish to go back home, especially with Steve on the prowl. So we drank some more.... And then called the police.

I came round from my drunken haze in a police interview room with my mum and dad, along with Clare's mum, standing over us.

'What do you think you're doing?' said Clare's mum, 'you are so grounded for this!'

And it was true. Clare was grounded. Forced to go to school the next day, despite the hangover. Her mobile phone confiscated.

Dad did something rather different. He bought me a new phone. He let me stay home from school. He seemed basically to be rewarding me for my running away.

I took advantage.

Found Out

There was a limit to what even Dad would allow. My behaviour was becoming so much wilder. Staying out through the nights, I skipped school. Hanging around with Pete, Adam and Craig wasn't good for me either. These were three mixed up boys.

More often than not, we found ourselves in squatters' flats, drinking and smoking cannabis. There were plenty of others there, most of them older than us, many of them using heroin and cocaine, and engaging in casual sex. We joined in.

I used to chat up the security guard to one of the set of flats we went to. I wish I hadn't. One day, he called me into his office and sexually assaulted me. The police found out, but I refused to say anything.

Dad was worried by my absences. Hasan had been over to see me and, with me not having been home at all that particular day, the two of them decided to find me. We heard the police coming. My friends escaped out of a window. I just sat there, smoking cannabis. They could catch me if they wanted, I didn't care. A police cell might be better than the streets anyway.

Dad was with the police. I was taken home and left in my bedroom to sleep off the effects.

Breaking Up

I didn't really like Hasan that much. He was from Bangladesh and, despite pulling away from his Muslim traditions, he was still very much engaged with that community. He was four years older and in that sense, a more appropriate boyfriend than Steve. I remember sitting down with Emma at the church youth group and asking her what I should do. I'm not sure she gave me the best advice.

'What do you want to do, Selina? Which one do you love?'

I didn't love either. I wasn't sure I believed in love. Love was for other people, not me. Love was for a child who had a mother. I was simply accepting any relationship that came along, anyone that would show me interest, anything to fill the deep emptiness

I felt inside. I needed God's unconditional love. Instead, I was accepting conditional, controlling manipulation. To my twisted thinking, you accepted the love you thought you deserved.

Things came to a head with Steve in a nasty way. We were out walking on a winter's day. He'd bought me a ring and in one of our arguments, I threw it away into the snow. He was so angry, shouting and swearing. During that time, Steve became more violent and would often hit me. Another time we were out walking and arguing. Steve got so irate, he grabbed me around the throat and began to shake me. By now we were on a bridge over a busy road. I really thought he was going to throw me off. Instead, he grabbed hold of my Walkman, complete with earphones and CD, and threw them over the bridge into the oncoming traffic.

Things ended then. Not that there was a date I left him. In fact, I remember still being with him on occasions after that. But there were other men taking over. More my age. Less controlling.

Hospital

I was still only fourteen years old. The emotion of dealing with Steve was too much for me. I began to think again about suicide. And this time I tried harder.

I drank a bottle of vodka. I emptied a pack of paracetamol down my throat. I cut my wrists.

I ended up in a secure hospital unit, with my shoelaces taken out of my trainers. Mum and Dad visited. Hasan visited too. He was angry with me.

'Why?! Why are you doing these things, Selina?'

The truth is, I didn't really know. Craig had recently been abused by another man. Adam was depressed and talking of suicide. Pete talked openly of ways to end it all. My street friends were definitely an influence, and not a good one.

Trips to psychiatrists followed. It didn't do any good. I refused to take part.

I still carry the scars on my wrists.

Night Driving

Sex, alcohol and cannabis were the constants in the months that followed. I was getting deeper into the drug culture, smoking cannabis whenever I could, and still hanging round with Pete, Adam and Craig. With the drink and drugs came more casual sex. Men picked me up. Friends of friends. I was raped on more than one occasion. But despite the men, it all kept coming back to Hasan. He continued to look out for me and seemed to genuinely care. He disliked my chosen street friends and on at least one occasion, took a rather frightened Adam in his car and abandoned him in the middle of a field in the countryside.

What started as a friendship, and the occasional rescue mission, morphed into a relationship. We would drive around in his Vauxhall Astra convertible, and I enjoyed it. Visits to Lichfield and Tamworth nearby. Pleasant towns, places I'd never been to. Clare would come along as well sometimes. Fast driving, loud music, it was a lot of fun.

Our romance was managed over some strange hours. Hasan worked in his uncle's Indian restaurant, so was often leaving work at around midnight.

I'd regularly say goodnight to Mum and Dad, wait until they were asleep and then slip out of the front door, walking to the petrol station nearby. There, I would wait for Hasan to arrive.

Night driving was common, but so was going to bed. We used a property his parents owned nearby. Most of the time it was empty, but if any of Hasan's family came over, we had to make a quick escape. One of Hasan's brothers was training to be an Imam. He was strict on what was and was not allowed. If I had been caught with Hasan, we would both have been punished. Hasan could well have lost his life in what was called an 'honour killing', due to his bringing shame on the family.

I had to hide in the boot of Hasan's car one time when he unexpectedly was asked to pick up his brother from the Imam training school in Kidderminster. Kidderminster to Walsall is the best part of an hour's drive. It was hard to stay quiet. And harder still to stay in the car boot.

Another time, Hasan saw a cousin in the distance as we walked down the high street.

'Selina, walk behind me! Quickly! Walk behind!'

Walking behind a Muslim husband may be common in their culture. But this was much more basic. Walking behind a Muslim boyfriend in order that no one from Hasan's community would notice.

First Wife

It had been a fun evening driving around Lichfield when eventually Hasan pulled up at the petrol station near our house. I kissed him goodbye, but this time, he didn't let me go.

'Selina, can I ask you... would you... would you consider being my first wife?'

'What? First wife? What do you mean?'

'What I say. I think you're so beautiful. I want you to be my first wife.'

'I get the wife bit, Hasan. It's the *first* bit I don't get. What do you mean?'

'Oh. Yes. I see. In my tradition, there can be more than one wife. My family has plans for me to marry someone from Bangladesh and bring her back to the country.'

'I can't believe you are saying these things, Hasan! I'm not going to be anyone's *first* wife! If I find the right man, I'll be his *only* wife, I'll be the love of his life. But I can tell you one thing... It's not going to be you!'

I pulled myself away from him, got out of the car and slammed the door.

What a jerk! First wife no less! It was hard to believe. I thought he had loved me and now he was marrying someone else.

I wasn't sure trying to keep this relationship was worth the stress. But that changed the day I found out I was pregnant.

Miscarriage

We weren't being careful enough. No managed birth control. No real thought to the consequences. But there we were. He was nineteen. I was still fourteen.

The pregnancy only lasted a matter of weeks.

It ended in a miscarriage. My parents protected me. They didn't tell the school the reason I was at home in bed.

It took a while to recover. Emotionally as much as physically.

Hasan was noticeable by his absence at this time. He didn't want to get involved with me while I was still in bed and simply asked my mum to tell him when I was better. I should have seen the warning signs. If a man is not there when you most need him, how is the relationship going to last?

But I was under Hasan's spell by this point. I can't say that I loved him, but he brought a sense of stability into my life. He was a protector—well, most of the time, ignoring his absence during the miscarriage.

'They're no good for you, Selina. I don't want you to see them again.'

Hasan was talking about Pete, Adam and Craig of course. But also Clare. Hasan saw her as a bad influence and, despite the years of friendship, I went along with him. I cut myself off from them all.

This wasn't entirely a bad thing. It meant I stopped smoking cannabis, and I began drinking a lot less too.

It also meant that my school grades began to improve again. Cannabis was having a severe affect on my education. From being one of the brightest in the school, I became someone who simply didn't care, who refused to do the homework, who daydreamed through the classes. Or who became deliberately rude and provocative in the hope I was thrown out of class. It worked too. I was kicked out of science classes, geography and religious education.

At one point, I ended up doing all my school work in the head of year's office, as none of the teachers wanted me disrupting their classes.

That's if I went at all of course. On occasion, I would just stay away, hanging around the town centre, smoking the cannabis that my dad was buying for me. Not that I was in the least appreciative of Dad's actions—in addition to the money he gave me for drugs, I stole more from his wallet anyway, spending it on alcohol and cigarettes.

So, Hasan's influence was welcomed by my parents—and by the school, as I returned to the hard-working pupil I had been before.

But Hasan was also very controlling. As weeks turned to months, I found he was really the only person I was meeting up with. He'd cut me off from my other friends, he'd stopped me visiting The Vine and hanging around on the streets. Trips out were with him alone.

It was controlling, but in a way, I felt secure. Coming off cannabis was a significant turning point for me. It meant that I could have gone in a new direction. I could have become one of the top students. I could have gone back to church with Clare. I could have become a more responsible child for my parents.

But then, Aisha arrived.

The New Mum

It wasn't long after announcing to Hasan that I was pregnant again that he disappeared from the scene. Hasan went to Bangladesh to get married.

Alone, aged fifteen, and pregnant. I was scared. Faisal called round to see how I was doing. Faisal was Hasan's cousin and had been the one to tell me about Hasan's disappearance to Bangladesh. He seemed to truly care and shared his concern for me being on my own.

Mum and Dad were as helpful as they could be in nursing me through my pregnancy. But the thing is, they had not had any children themselves and felt as much adrift as I did.

I remember the day it happened as if it was yesterday. I was lying on my bed, watching television. Kate Winslet and Leonardo DiCaprio were just about to enact the scene in *Titanic* where they stand at the bow of the ship. I looked down. I was wearing my Kappa white jogging bottoms with the blue stripe. Except they were no longer white. Blood was seeping down my leg. Mum and Dad rushed me over to the hospital. By the time we got there, there was a pool of blood on the floor of the car. I don't remember much else. The doctors put me to sleep and gave me a blood transfusion. I was a week or so in the hospital and thankfully the baby was saved, still in my womb and able to go full term.

Those final few months are all a bit of a blur. I stayed in bed for a lot of that time, concerned that I would lose the baby. Mum and Dad were extra attentive and Faisal called round most days.

Aisha arrived at the end of January. I was sixteen.

Chapter Four

One Too Many

It's not meant as an excuse, really it isn't. But being adopted can just be hard work. No matter how much my mum and dad loved me, there was always that emptiness, always that feeling of rejection. It played out in different ways. Anger and rebellion in my early teens through to a desperate insecurity and a need to be loved as I got older.

Aisha brought a sense of purpose. There was somebody I needed to love and in return, I felt her unconditional love for me. On the one hand, I was so unprepared for motherhood, but on the other hand, it brought a fulfilment and purpose that I had lacked.

Not that this was my first reaction after the baby was born.

Emotions

Hasan, Aisha's father, was still in Bangladesh. Faisal was there, pretty much a constant in my life at that time. Mum stayed with me at the hospital for as long as she could but, in the end, she was told to go home.

As she walked out of the door, all my emotions came to the surface. Suddenly, I felt abandoned. I was only sixteen years old with a baby in my arms. I didn't even know how to hold her! I'm not sure who cried more—me or Aisha.

Back home, things were better. Mum settled me into bed and between us, we cared for baby Aisha over those first few months. I remember the first time Mum and Dad went out, leaving me alone with her. I panicked.

'Mum, it's me. It's Aisha—I'm not sure she's breathing!'

'Calm down, Selina. Just put your hand next to her face and see if you can feel her breath.'

I did and of course Aisha was absolutely fine.

The Return

There was a knock at the door.

'Selina! You've got a visitor! Hasan is here.'

Once again, my emotions were all over the place. I wasn't sure what to expect. Aisha was about to meet her father for the first time, and I had no idea how he would react.

His body language, as he came through the door, was somewhat downbeat.

'Hi.'

'Hello.'

Hasan walked over to the bed, leaning over to look at the tiny baby in my arms. He slowly reached out to touch her head and stroke her face, before sitting on the edge of the bed.

'She's beautiful.'

'Yes, she is.'

'Selina, I've got some news. I'm married. She's not here yet—she's still in Bangladesh, but I hope she'll be coming over in the next few months once we sort the paperwork.'

It was so matter of fact. I wasn't sure how to react.

'Well, I have some news too . . .'

And with that, I launched into something of a confession regarding my relationship with Faisal. Hasan's response was a bit of a surprise. Because of his own news, I wasn't sure he would even care. But he did care. He seemed genuinely upset that I had got so close to someone else. His reaction was enough to throw me off a bit, leaving me confused.

Over the next few weeks, Hasan was a regular visitor. Aware that Hasan was back, Faisal didn't call. Slowly, I fell back into my old relationship. I can't say that I loved him, but it simply happened.

Hasan showed me genuine care but didn't appear to be so loving towards our baby. I later learnt that this was likely a reflection of his own upbringing. Within his community, traditionally, a girl was not particularly valued, and he was keen to have a son.

Three months later, I was pregnant again. A year and five days after Aisha's birth, Hasan had his son—Arun arrived.

Violence

That year, between the two babies, was not without its moments. It seems to me now that Hasan came from a particularly traditional family and within that culture, not only were women seen as second class, but violence towards them was acceptable.

It started with a misunderstanding.

One day, Hasan came storming into the house, running up the stairs. As the door was flung open, he began to scream at me.

'What do you mean by calling the restaurant every few minutes?!'

'I haven't called.'

'Don't lie! I know it must have been you. Somebody phoning and complaining about me. Not just the once, but again and again through the day. To my uncle! You should never do that. Don't talk to my family. What you did is shameful.'

'But I didn't! I haven't called anybody.'

'Don't lie!'

My dad had been building a new wardrobe in my bedroom. Hasan picked up one of the pieces of wood and began to slam it against my legs. Hearing my screams, Dad came into the bedroom.

'What's going on? What are you doing? Stop that! Get out of here!'

The police were called. Even then, Hasan felt he was in the right, explaining to the police that it was appropriate for him to punish me in this way. The police asked him to leave.

Challenging

Despite the violence, that wasn't the end of the relationship. There was something in me that still appreciated Hasan being around. His control over me was almost something I wanted. Aware of my past, aware of the countless times I was out of control on drugs or alcohol, I felt the need for that control. Especially now that Aisha was with us. I wanted to be the best of mums for her and that meant no more drugs and no more alcohol. By staying within Hasan's control, I could manage my cravings and accept that it was best to stay at home with my child and with little or no contact with the outside world.

Hasan was still very much part of my life until shortly before the birth of Arun. But it was noticeable around that time that his visits to the house became less and less. I wasn't sure why, but was determined to find out. I managed to speak to Hasan's sister-in-law one afternoon, only to find out that Hasan was, at that moment, at Walsall Manor Hospital, awaiting the birth of his first child with his Bangladeshi wife.

Something inside me exploded.

Leaving the children in Mum's care, I raced over to the hospital. On entering the maternity ward, there in front of me was Hasan together with his mother, brothers and sisters. I went for it.

'You little piece of s***! What do you think you're doing?! What about your other children? You can't just wander off and leave us! How dare you run away!'

The family managed to calm me down and eventually, Hasan took me outside the hospital. What happened next was something I simply was not anticipating. He beat me up. Thankfully, one of the security guards noticed what was happening and came to my rescue.

Needless to say, Aisha and Arun's father no longer appeared in our lives so frequently from that point on. Even then, I didn't exactly end the relationship, but I knew it had to end. There had been one too many women in Hasan's life. I was the casualty.

Belonging

I wanted to belong. I wanted people around me who cared for me. But every relationship seemed to turn abusive. Love that may have been shown at first, morphed into control and manipulation. Was I asking for too much? Was it too much to ask for someone who just loved me for who I was?

But then again, who was I? Some adopted kid without any kind of understanding as to her identity. Unsure even of her parents' love. Controlled by her dad as much as by other men. Giving away her body to men in the hope of love. In the hope of love, of care, of protection.

And still in the back of my mind was an awareness of God. The letters to God were no more, but the conversations continued. God, if you are there, then why … Why the abuse? Why the lack of control? Why that unfulfilled need to be loved?

Chapter Five

Six Children by Twenty

'Clare, he's suffocating me! He's got a wife from Bangladesh, he keeps hitting me and he still expects me to do everything he wants me to do. I really can't cope with it.'

'Then why don't you come out with me?'

I screamed into the phone. 'Because he'll still find me!'

'So how about you end it? For goodness' sake, Selina, he's married to another woman. You don't owe him anything. You shouldn't even be with him. Especially with the way he's been treating you.'

I threw my mobile phone to the floor. What had my life become? A recluse while Hasan was 'managing' me. And when he wasn't around, just the daily pressures of looking after two kids.

Mum and Dad were keen for me to have some kind of social life, so they and Clare wore me down in the end. I agreed to a trip to the local Wetherspoons pub.

The Dare

I sat at a table with Clare and some of her gay friends. Except that one of them obviously was not gay. His name was Darren and he kept looking in my direction.

'I dare you! Go on! Ask him out!'

That was Clare of course. A little the worse for drink and, as often happened when the two of us were together, things would get out of control. We loved provoking each other to do outrageous things.

So, I did. I asked him out.

He was a nice man, about my age. Not much to look at but with a pleasant smile. We exchanged phone numbers and soon after, started dating. It was mainly visits to local pubs. This included the Golden Lion in Walsall, a gay bar where we could usually find Clare. Not that Darren was very comfortable with being ogled by the security guards on our way in!

Things developed slowly with Darren. I remember the day, early on in our relationship, when I explained to him that I had two children.

'Yes, Aisha is just over one year old, and Arun is three months.'

'Three months? You had a baby three months ago?!'

'Yes. That's why he's three months.' Said with a smile.

Despite these revelations, Darren was still keen to date me.

It wasn't long, of course, before Darren found out about Hasan. He wasn't happy about it and forced me to drive him over to the restaurant. Before I knew it, the two were exchanging blows.

Hasan really was reluctant to let go. One night he called round, and I went for a walk with him. It wasn't quite the pleasant stroll I had imagined. He was brutal. Physically aggressive and verbally demanding. I'd had enough.

A relationship that should have ended months before ended that night.

Remarkably – amusingly when I look back – Hasan continued a relationship with Mum and Dad. He even called round on Mum for a cup of tea occasionally and that friendship continued through to my mum's death. Hasan was a strange man. One moment very loving and honourable, the next incredibly aggressive and controlling.

The same could not be said of Darren.

Sophie

It was simply part of my life that anybody I dated would also end up in my bed. I was pregnant with Sophie not long after the start of my relationship with Darren.

He was really sweet about it, excited to be a father. Maybe a bit immature as well. He mentioned more than once that he wanted us to have a baby so that one of the children would be his.

I was still living at home with Mum and Dad, and it wasn't long before Darren moved in. Mum and Dad were a bit concerned but perhaps, compared to some of my previous relationships, this one seemed more stable.

I do remember Darren moving out as well though. For a while, he went back to live with his mum. At the time I thought little of it, but looking back, there were telltale signs that he was unsure about our relationship. He seemed to get moody and withdrawn, to the extent that one day his mother came to our front door. She was angry and telling Mum that I should get an abortion, that Darren didn't want any children and that it was a complete mistake.

He got over it though and it wasn't long before he was back living with me, alongside Mum and Dad. But if I had paid attention, the signals were already there that this was just another relationship and not one that was going to last.

I did appreciate, though, that life was a little more normal than in my previous relationships. Darren was just a good normal guy. Strangely, he liked to go to bingo. This was certainly a far cry from my days on the streets, smoking cannabis and getting drunk!

A printer by trade, Darren was a little deaf and had hearing aids in both ears. I guess he wasn't that much to look at, but he seemed to care. We hardly ever argued, and he was never physically abusive. All this was an enormous 'plus' as far as I was concerned. Up until this point in time, I really hadn't had what could be called a normal relationship. I had no real concept as to what a normal relationship was.

Darren was a good dad as well. Aisha and Arun loved being around him. He was more of a dad to them than their actual father. I appreciated his care.

Sophie arrived eighteen months after Arun. The twins, Megan and Tegan, arrived nine months after Sophie.

Yes, you read that correctly.

Premature

Following Sophie's birth, I quickly became pregnant again. The hospital scan showed that this was twins. I shouldn't have been surprised. Darren is a twin. His mother is a twin. His grandmother is a twin.

All went well with this pregnancy until the six-month mark. I woke up one morning feeling weaker than usual. I sensed something wasn't right and eventually persuaded my dad to take me over to the hospital. The tests revealed that 'baby two' had a very low heart rate.

'Selina, this is dangerous,' said the doctor, 'we need to get you into surgery straight away. We need to do an emergency C section'

I had arrived at the hospital around 10.30 in the morning. Megan was born at 11.41 am and one minute later, Tegan arrived.

Hospital Time

To the mothers reading this, you will understand that you will do anything for your children. What followed the birth of the twins was one of the craziest and most demanding times in my life.

The twins needed to stay in hospital for quite a while. They both dropped below their birth weight to approximately two pounds each. In addition, Megan developed encephalitis—a swelling on the brain. At one point, she was moved from Walsall Manor Hospital to the main children's hospital in Birmingham.

Not to be outdone, Tegan picked up an infection as well and, still below her birth weight, this was a concern.

At the same time, Arun became ill with a water infection and ended up on the emergency children's ward. Aisha was not particularly well back at home and Sophie was still a young baby as well of course.

Each day revolved around driving to Walsall Manor Hospital (and occasionally the Children's Hospital, Birmingham) three times a day and dashing home in between times in order to look after Aisha and Sophie.

I wasn't well myself, having picked up an infection from the surgery.

It was one of those times when you don't really have time to stop and think. You just keep going. Strictly speaking, I wasn't allowed to drive so soon after the C-section surgery, but I had to. Mum and Dad were as supportive as possible, as was Darren when he was home from work.

After three months in hospital, the twins were able to come home. They still had heart monitors attached to them which we needed to keep in place for some time, but to all intents and purposes, we were a family together again.

They were crazy days. I'm only glad that in every case, there was a full recovery. All five children were back home with us. And we were still living in Mum and Dad's house. My brother Anthony was at home and had his own bedroom. Sophie and the twins slept with us. Aisha and Arun were in Mum and Dad's bedroom. Really, this couldn't last!

And then . . . Thirteen months after the birth of the twins, Reece arrived.

I was twenty years old. With six children.

Five days before Christmas, while I was still pregnant with Reece, Darren went to work. And didn't come back.

Alone

He'd planned it. I had no idea. When I knew I was pregnant with Reece, Darren and I had had a difficult conversation. He wanted me to have an abortion. I refused. The thought of six children played on Darren's mind. There were no big bust ups, no massive arguments, but I could see he was growing distant, distracted.

What I didn't know was that he had planned his escape.

That evening, five days before Christmas, I can remember the number of times I looked up at the kitchen clock. Still no Darren. One by one, Mum and I sorted the kids out and got them to bed. Still no Darren.

There was a knock at the door in the early evening. It was Darren's mum. We invited her in and with a mug of tea in hand and a smug look on her face, she told us the news.

'He's not coming back. He's had enough. Darren can't take the stress of the relationship, of all the children. He's got on a train and he's not coming back.'

It turns out the last bit about the train was a lie. With help from his mum, Darren had rented a flat just five minutes away.

It's only when you look back, you see the signs. He announced that he was selling his beloved stereo system to a friend at work and took it with him a few days before he left. Of course, it was a lie. He wanted the stereo with him in his new flat. Some of his clothes had been smuggled out and there were other signs of preparation if you looked for them. But I didn't look for them. I had no idea.

Numb at the thought of being alone, facing Christmas on my own, staring at each of my children as they slept that evening, I cried. What was I going to do? How had it got to this? A mother with six children. The fathers gone. Alone.

I cried.

Six children and only twenty. How had it come to this?

If there was ever a God, I needed him now.

Chapter Six

The Stalker

'Mummy, where is daddy Darren?'

'He's not here, my love. But we're okay. It's Christmas Day! Look what Father Christmas got you!'

And with that, the older children began to open their presents.

I held back the tears. For the sake of the children, I had to stay strong. I had to hold it together. But inside, it was turmoil.

Abandoned. Angry. Alone. Five children to care for and one more on the way.

Challenge

I wasn't about to give up on Darren, though. He was the father of three of my children and with another on the way, how could he do this to me?! Just to walk out, with no warning, no explanation. It was simply too much.

Soon after Christmas, I turned up on the steps of Darren's printing company. He was there but refused to speak to me. His sister came round, threatening to beat me up. I was about six months pregnant with Reece at the time, so her comments were almost laughable.

But I got the message. He wasn't coming home.

Until he did come home.

New Year's Eve was when the text arrived. We spent the evening in Darren's flat with him apologising and saying he'd got it wrong. He wanted to be with me after all.

I'm not sure how I felt, to be honest. He left. Now he was back. Mum and Dad weren't much help either.

'He's not coming back here! I won't let him in!'

That was Dad.

'He can't possibly love you after all he's done. Selina, are you really sure you want to reopen that relationship? You must be crazy if you think you can trust him.'

That was Mum.

In the end, Darren changed his mind again. I don't know how much of it was Mum and Dad affecting his thinking. For my part, I would have had him back.. But it wasn't to be.

As I was trying to deal with Darren, Clare was dealing with me.

'Stop it, Selina! Just stop it! I know it's bad but sitting there all day just isn't right. Come on, let me take you to the pub. Your mum and dad won't mind looking after the kids for a while.'

And that is how I met the stalker.

Mister Smooth

'Hey ladies, how are we doing tonight?'

He was a bit of a looker. Someone who obviously worked out in the gym. Dark spiky hair reflecting his half English, half Jamaican heritage. A goatee beard. Smelling of aftershave and dressed smartly – suit and tie – quite the charmer. A fair bit older than me, but still with boyish good looks.

'Here's my business card. I help run a limo company. I'm the best driver there is—if you ladies fancy a night out on the town, give me a call. I won't disappoint!'

I wasn't interested.

'In fact, tell you what, give me your phone number and I'll take you out anyway. On the house. My treat. Call it a date if you like.'

The whole thing felt a little bit déjà vu. This was the Malthouse, the same Wetherspoons pub that I'd met Darren in. The same friend with me that evening.

His comments were directed at me. I couldn't understand how he was even attracted, bearing in mind I was around seven months pregnant by then. I thought the charm was totally over the top. He was just too smooth. A bit of a player with all the girls. Someone to be avoided.

I declined. What I didn't know was that Clare passed my number on to him anyway.

The text arrived the very next day. His name was Eddie. Could we meet up?

I didn't really mind him contacting me and was happy for him to call round at first. Dad wanted to know why an old man was wanting to talk to me. An old man! Well, he was eighteen years older than me, so fair enough.

I still wasn't interested in any kind of relationship. I suspected he had a number of girls. I certainly didn't want to be one of that number. So, I ignored the majority of the texts that kept arriving. I pretended to be out when he called around the house.

He was never impolite, never aggressive at this time, but it was strange that he wanted to pay me so much attention when I had made it clear I was not interested in a relationship. He wasn't one to give up though. The texts became more insistent and more frequent. He started turning up outside the house.

It was a bit of a joke at first—Dad started calling him 'the stalker'. It was only later that I began to realise that this was exactly what he was.

Drinking Again

With Reece's arrival, I was able to start drinking again. I took the opportunity with both hands—and with my lips. My twenty-first birthday party was a pub crawl around Birmingham. Clare and her friends challenged me to kiss twenty-one people to celebrate the day. Strangers in a nightclub. Men and women. Nevertheless, I took the dare.

Visits to the pub became a regular occurrence, usually with Clare. But the other regular factor was Eddie. He became our usual driver when Clare and I were out drinking.

It was drinking that started the relationship with Eddie. I had continued to ignore him and hardly ever answered the ten to twenty texts that he sent each day. But he continued to work as a driver for myself and Clare when we went out. One night I was particularly drunk, and it was Eddie who picked me up. Two hours later I arrived home. My conclusion was simple—we had become intimate on that journey home and he must therefore be my boyfriend. It was logical. It wasn't emotional.

Once again, I had simply walked into a relationship without thinking of the consequences and with no real love for the man that I was with.

And that's how it happened. The stalker became the lover.

What I didn't know was that I had just started a relationship that would leave me in the darkest of places. I had no idea at the time, but Darren and Hasan in comparison were complete angels.

They're Coming to Get Me

All the warning signs were there. On my first visit to his house, I met his youngest daughter and learnt about his ex. It turns out that they were still in touch. And then there was his ex-girlfriend, Allie. He assured me that the relationship was over, but I wasn't entirely convinced.

Relationships were clearly still an issue but what I particularly remember from that first visit were the drugs.

Eddie was getting high on LSD. I had been with him for most of that first day and with no need to get back to the kids with Mum in charge, I stayed on. And observed the drug taking. He even offered me some, but I wasn't interested. It was the middle of the night when the noise began.

I awoke to find Eddie in the corner of the bedroom, back against the wall, screaming.

'They're coming for me, Selina, they're coming for me. They're demons! They're coming to get me. Stop them! Stop them!'

I calmed him, sat him on the bed and brought him down from his trip, holding his hand.

It turns out he was seeing demons pretty much all the time. What had I started? What was I letting myself in for with this relationship? He was eighteen years older. He had a young daughter and was still in contact with his ex-girlfriend. He had two children from a previous relationship and had been banned from seeing them. And he was hallucinating on LSD.

Any sane woman would have walked away. Maybe I was as crazy as him. I stayed.

Suicide Attempt

I was at home putting the kids to bed when the call came through.

'Selina, I'm sorry. I've been seeing Allie. She's told me she's had enough, and I know you have too. So this is goodbye. I've just taken a pile of stuff. I'm sorry, babe, but that's it.'

And with that, he hung up.

Dad and I dashed round to the house. Kicking in the bedroom door, Dad dragged Eddie off the floor and onto the bed. The ambulance came in time.

Driving back home, Dad was giving me one of those looks. I knew what was coming.

'Selina, this really isn't good for you. He's nearly old enough to be your own father. He's just tried to take his life because of a relationship with another woman. Get out of it! Get out of it before it gets too crazy.'

'You're right, Dad, I know I should.'

But I didn't.

I craved relationships. They were my particular drug. To be loved, physically and emotionally, was what I lived for. I didn't like the man, but I couldn't let go of the relationship.

The manipulation was fairly subtle at first.

'Hey, babe, you don't mind, do you? I'm feeling so tired. Just this once?'

And so I became the main means of transport for Eddie's three children. What started as helping out 'just the once' quickly became the pattern.

With no real job other than occasional limousine work, Eddie would spend many days lying in bed taking drugs. He wasn't really caring for me and didn't seem to love me. I still wasn't sure that his relationship with Allie was completely over. But I let our relationship continue. And as it continued, things got darker.

Chapter Seven

Cuckoo in the Nest

Pete and Diane were good friends of Eddie's. I liked them too. We used to go on fishing trips together to a local lake, spending the day smoking cannabis and catching an occasional bream.

On one occasion Eddie and I had had an argument, so I was sitting further round the lake on my own. Eddie didn't like it and was shouting at me to come back. His constant anger was becoming more of an issue. He got so angry that he threw a bottle of Lucozade at me. He was a good shot—it hit me in the side.

Back home, I began to feel unwell. It just got worse and worse. After three days of increasing pain, Dad came over and he and Diane took me to the Accident and Emergency Department at the hospital. They couldn't find anything at first, but the pain grew in intensity and eventually I was sedated. Twenty-four hours later, there was a doctor leaning over my bed as I came round, explaining that I had a ruptured spleen and was lucky to still be alive. The Lucozade bottle was the culprit.

Clare and Mum were the first to visit me.

'You have to get away from him', said Clare, 'He's messing you up.'

If only I had listened. I didn't listen for thirteen years. Thirteen years with a monster.

Surprise, Surprise…

In amongst the craziness, there was a bright moment. At long last, the council had managed to find me my own home. I was so excited. The children and I would be able to make a fresh start. It was just around the corner from my mum and dad so they would still be able to support me. An ideal solution.

Leaving hospital after fifteen days, I wasn't quite sure what was happening when Eddie welcomed me back to my new house.

'Hey babe, surprise! I've moved in! I've left the old house—couldn't manage the rent, to be honest. But this will be great, won't it? We can all be together!'

I was in shock. This was my house and there was someone else living there. A cuckoo in the nest.

As I walked into the lounge, his furniture greeted me. This was wrong! So wrong. This was my house. I wanted to be the one to choose the furniture, to paint the walls. But I couldn't argue. I was feeling physically weak and the best I could do was to climb the stairs and lie down.

There was another surprise to come. In the middle of the night, my first night out of hospital, Eddie woke up clutching his chest.

He was sick and shaking. I wondered whether it was drugs related and called an ambulance. A good job I did.

It was a heart attack.

The instructions from my doctor were to take things easy in order to ensure that I healed properly, but here I was, within a few days, pushing Eddie around in a wheelchair as he recovered from having had a stent fitted. It turns out this is a rather appropriate picture for the whole of our relationship.

Hanging Around

Those early days with Eddie were all a bit strange. Eddie didn't have any regular employment but the bits he did do – driving the limousine mainly – were for an Asian businessman called Ahmed. We would hang out at Ahmed's shop. Ahmed sold the best mobile phones around at that time. In fact, they were so good, we used to hang them around our necks to show them off. They were the first ones with colour screens and we were very excited that they even had a game called 'snakes' that we could play!

Hanging around meant smoking cannabis and accompanying Eddie with his driving. I'd sit with him as a passenger on the front seat, whilst we transported clients.

One day, Ahmed had had way too much to drink and on the spur of the moment, decided to close up the shop and ask one of the drivers to take him, his girlfriend, me and Eddie out for the day. We drove all the way to North Wales and nearly got stuck on the

Llanberis pass. By the end of the day, I was the only passenger not drunk and the only person able to direct the driver.

Ahmed was part of a close-knit Asian community. There was a degree of hostility between various Asian groups, often ending up in gang fights. Ahmed was asked by some of his cousins to help them with a particularly troubling individual. He ended up hitting the man with a baseball bat and killing him. Ahmed ran for his life to Pakistan and didn't come back.

The problem was that the police didn't fully believe it was only Ahmed who was involved. They had it in mind that Eddie had also taken part. This was not at all true as Eddie had been with me that day and had nothing to do with it. But the police were not taking 'no' for an answer and were continually pestering me to 'confess' that Eddie had actually been involved as well. It didn't help that the police dogs could smell drugs on me. Most of the time, I was carrying drugs for Eddie, fearful that if I didn't have them on me and available to him at all times, he might flare up and hit me—something that was beginning to happen with increasing frequency.

I felt I couldn't even speak to Eddie about the police questions as, with his temper, he would have gone straight to the police station and got himself into trouble. And worse, he may well have started hitting me, accusing me of speaking to the police, despite not admitting anything to them. Nor could I mention to the police what I knew of Ahmed. His cousins were making it very clear that if I said anything, I wouldn't live to see my children grow up.

In the end, the stress drove me to the doctors. Along with the cannabis, I began to take a cocktail of antidepressants.

Anger

I was getting stressed and Eddie was getting worse. He would flare up at the smallest of things. Within a few months of being together, there were holes and dents in many of the walls where Eddie had smashed his fists into them. A lot of the furniture ended up broken where he had taken his anger out on it. One time, he threw a chair through the back window, angry at some trivial mistake I appeared to have made.

The police were regular visitors. Often, they had been called by one of the neighbours, hearing the screaming and the blazing rows. I tried to give as good as I got, but Eddie was far too strong for me. Over my thirteen years with Eddie, I can remember broken ribs, black eyes, and bruises pretty much all over my body. On more than one occasion, he tried to strangle me. I'm only alive because a friend of Eddie's pulled him away one time, when it really could have been fatal.

Another time, he knocked a tooth out. He would immediately become very apologetic and even cry after these attacks. Most of the time I'd just tell him where to go, whilst tending my wounds.

Eddie would become angry at the slightest thing and was extremely jealous of any other men who dared to talk to me. On one occasion, I was simply looking out of the car window whilst a man walked past. Eddie slapped me in the face and started screaming, accusing me of looking at other men. I'd had enough so got out of the car and started to walk away.

'Where are you going? Come back, you b****.'

He started to run after me. I sped up but could not escape. As he grabbed hold of me, he twisted my arm, pulling me into his grip. Squeezing me close, I felt my ribs break.

Just another set of injuries to add to the list. Just another argument for no particular reason. Just the way it was.

The violence became constant. When it first began, I remember feeling frightened. But somehow, I got to the point where I really didn't care. It was just life. Physical abuse, sexual abuse, verbal abuse, accusations, mind games. That was Eddie.

Prisoner

One of Eddie's little games was to check my mobile. He'd go through any calls that I'd made and if they weren't to Mum and Dad, he'd start asking questions or accusing me of talking to other men. It got to the point where it was simply easier not to call anyone. I became more and more of a recluse, a prisoner in my own home.

Early on in our relationship, Eddie made it clear that it would be me financing everything. I paid the rent on the house, the tax on the car. I paid for our holidays, including paying for his own children. For most of our relationship, he had very little income and the small amount he did earn, he spent on himself. But it wasn't the financial abuse that was the worst.

Most days, I'd wake up in the morning wondering, not *whether* Eddie would be hitting me today, but *when*. I'd try and prepare my mind for the mental tortures that would await me the moment I walked into the kitchen for my morning bottle of Lucozade. I drank about six bottles of Lucozade a day at this time. Another addiction really, but better than some.

I would try and plan to avoid Eddie as much as possible, hoping that he would want to play Call of Duty on his Xbox, which he did for hours on end. At the same time, I felt totally dependent upon him. To ease the pain, both physical and mental, I had increased my use of cannabis. And of course, it was Eddie who supplied me. I wasn't sure I could cope without it and therefore whether I could cope without him. What a way to live.

Sometimes, when the violence got so bad and I couldn't endure any more, I'd run away. I'd hide in amongst the bins, or around the corner against a wall, hoping against hope that Eddie wouldn't find me. This happened with increased regularity. Eddie would respond by getting into his car to drive around the estate searching for me.

Inevitably, I always had to come back to the house and face whatever physical abuse awaited me. And the crazy thing was, it was *my* house!

There was sexual abuse too. As far as Eddie was concerned, my body was his, to do with as he wished. And he wished a lot. This included taking videos to share with friends online and insisting that I carried out various sexual acts. At any point in time, he could insist on using me and abusing me. And he did.

The mind games that Eddie played were worse than anything that was physical or sexual. He would make you think that everything was your fault, and you'd believe him. If he forgot to buy a present for your birthday, it would be your fault for not reminding him. If you chose not to give him a gift, the consequences would be severe.

Always wanting to be the centre of attention, he would often cause arguments on special occasions such as my birthday, or even the children's birthdays, making out that we had wronged him in some way. It was all manipulation and incredibly narcissistic.

If I went out, he wanted to know where and who with. If he didn't know, he'd call me to find out. If I ignored the call, he'd keep calling. As many as fifty phone calls in succession until I eventually answered.

Thankfully, during the week, the children stayed with Mum and Dad for the most part, so they were sheltered from the torment. I saw them every day and, at the weekends, the kids would come over. For me, these were the best of times, as Eddie would try hard not to lose his temper. Despite this, my children still had to witness his screaming fits on occasion. It was even worse for his own children, with threats to kill himself, smashing up the house in front of them. Eddie even passed out a few times, so angry that he lost consciousness.

Patterns

I did fight back sometimes. Occasionally physically, not that this ever ended well. But there were times when I really had had enough and told Eddie to leave. I'd throw him out, but it wasn't long before the texts started arriving, pleading with me to let him back in, saying he had nowhere to live and didn't want to live without me, telling me he loved me. Foolishly, so often, I'd relent and invite him back.

The pattern would develop again. Constant verbal abuse. Physical abuse on a daily basis. Manipulation. Threats. And then again there would come a point where I had enough courage to throw him out of the house. Then, the texts.

One Sunday, things were really bad. We had a blazing argument and at one point, he stepped out of the front door to do something. I immediately slammed the door and locked it, then running to the back of the house to make sure that the kitchen door was locked as well. By the time I got back to the lounge, he had climbed through the back room window.

It was hard to sleep that night, the bruises covered my body and I couldn't move for the pain.

I was his slave, his prisoner. Eddie was always there. With his heart condition, he played the victim, often pretending to be ill when there was nothing wrong with him. He rarely left the house. He'd lie in bed most days, getting up to ask what was for dinner. If the reply was not appropriate, he would hit me. My whole life, day after day, revolved around survival. How to avoid making him angry. How to appease him. I'd do anything to keep him on side.

Frozen

As I became more and more the recluse, Mum was worried. She managed to get me out of the house one day and we had a great time going around the new art gallery in Walsall.

Returning home in the late afternoon, Eddie was still in bed. He was high on drugs and immediately started being abusive. Perhaps it was the contrast to the day I'd just had with Mum but instead of trying to avoid him, I just stood there and took it. What happened next was strange. I found that I couldn't move, my body was frozen. An ambulance came and eventually, I was diagnosed as having had a stress-induced mini stroke. Things really were getting serious.

Dad got the mental health crisis team involved at that point. I remember them sitting down with me in the lounge and me pleading with them to admit me to a psychiatric unit and section me.

'Just do it! Just section me. Take me away. I'm crazy. Put me away somewhere!'

Eddie was there though and persuaded the mental health team that he would be there to help me. I was given diazepam and my health records show me as having had a nervous breakdown.

I went in on myself all the more. The cocktail of drugs didn't help. But thankfully, something else happened. Eddie began to see that it wasn't going to last. He got himself a flat, although he still seemed to spend most of the time at my house.

One of the final events which caused me, at long last, to declare our relationship was over, concerned the children. It was Christmas 2013. Eddie had been drinking and came back late. His Christmas meal was spoiled because of it. However, this was not acceptable as far as Eddie was concerned and he threw his dinner across the kitchen.

This was too much for Arun and I witnessed a full-on fight between them. Even though Arun was only twelve, he fought crazily. The girls ran, hiding in the bathroom. Something of this event lodged in my brain and I realised it had to end.

Croatia

'Mum! Mum! It's the scouts. We're going to Croatia. Can I go? Please can I go? You can come too! Parents are allowed!'

And that's how I found myself on holiday in Croatia for ten days, alongside Arun.

It was while I was there that I began to realise just how crazy my life had become. The abuse had become so frequent, particularly the mental abuse, that I had genuinely begun to assume that this was the way life was for everybody. But the mums had another story.

'Selina! What are you doing?! How can you live like that? You need to get away from him. He's destroying you!'

Returning home after the trip, with the realisation that I could live without cannabis and that I could definitely live without Eddie, at long last I threw him out. For good.

The Doctors

Still fearful of Eddie, I changed the locks on the doors. I was so emotionally scarred by all that Eddie had done, it affected me to the extent that I had become a recluse; unwilling to leave the house, afraid to have any friends, scared of life itself. Enough to want to commit suicide.

Dad saw it for what it was and took me along to the doctors. It was as we walked in that I saw Eddie across the room. Immediately he got to his feet. I shrank back against Dad, aware of what was likely to happen.

'You b****! You complete ass****! You can't walk out on me! You're mine! I'm coming for you! I'll burn down your b***** house!'

And with that, he began to push me. Dad and one of the medical assistants held him back, but for the first time, he had been seen for what he was in public.

The police intervened. I took him to court to stop him from seeing the children. He broke the injunction. To court again. Again, he broke the injunction. For a third time, I was able to get an injunction against Eddie, and this time it worked. That was almost the last time I saw him actually, staring at me across the courtroom, mouthing swear words.

Thirteen years. Thirteen years of abuse. When Eddie had been high on drugs, he would often claim to see demons in the room. Looking back now, I think he was seeing something that was real. For thirteen years I lived with a man totally caught up with everything that was evil. But I chose to stay.

Why did I allow it? The effect on my children was considerable. The overall effect on me was that I had stopped living any kind of normal life.

And yet . . . I'd seen something different on that trip to Croatia. There was another way to live.

Chapter Eight

Discovering the Past

Hiding in my own home, fearful of going out, frightened of life itself, gave me a lot of time to think.

What was life about? Was it worth living? If it were not for the kids…

Adopted through a Catholic children's charity, brought up Catholic, I had a deeply rooted belief that if I was not good enough for God then I was not worth anything at all. I believed that my birth mother had not been good enough either and that is why God had taken me from her and placed me with a Catholic family. It was very confusing. On the one hand, I was told that God loved me so much that he placed me with a couple who could look after me but on the other hand, I believed that God didn't love me or my birth mum enough to keep us together.

Did he love me or didn't he? Was I worth anything or not?

But there were other thoughts too. Mum and Dad had always been very open about the fact that I was adopted. But it had been a 'closed adoption' (this is no longer allowed) where all my birth records had been destroyed.

Would I ever know who my birth mother was? Was there any way of finding out? Should I try?

I did actually have a name. As a teenager, I'd found a letter from the adoption agency which provided some minimum detail regarding the natural mothers of both myself and my adoptive brother Anthony.

The Argument

Perhaps inevitably, in the crazy times I was living in, my decision to find my real mum began with an argument. It was a full-on shouting match with my adopted mum. I can't quite remember the reasons for it now. More than likely, it would have been to do with Eddie.

But it was during that argument with Mum that she shouted these words:

'Why don't you stop the shouting? Why don't you leave me alone? Why don't you go and find your real mum?'

The words stayed with me. Why not try? But how?

Within a week of the argument with Mum, I had begun my search.

I knew I'd been born in Marston Green. And I knew my birth mother was called Monica Thompson. So, the first stop was Marston

Green Library. Did they have any kind of birth records or death records there? But the name was just too common. Who knew there were so many Monica Thompsons in one area?

The Cards

The next step was a phone call to the Father Hudson Children's Home. It had changed its name slightly, but I was able to find it. I explained that I was looking for my birth mum and they said they would contact me. Within a week, they called.

'Selina, we do have some information. I think it would be worth your while calling in.'

A few days later, I found myself sitting in the waiting room at the adoption agency. Having not yet split up at the time, Eddie was with me. And I was nervous.

'Come on through.'

The manager's smile was genuine, and my hopes rose just at that. Having sat down and ordered a cup of tea, the manager explained.

'This is most unusual, Selina. As you know, your adoption was under the old-fashioned system where we simply didn't keep any records. But something rather different has happened here.'

And with that, she lifted onto the desk two piles of envelopes. Each one was stamped and addressed to me, care of the agency.

The manager explained, 'It's unusual to hear from the birth mother again in this way, but in your case, she has sent you birthday cards and Christmas cards for every year of your life. Regulations didn't allow us to pass these on to you but now that you have inquired, here they are.'

Tears rolled down my face. All these years. And every year she had remembered me, she thought about me. Every year. Every year!

She loved me.

It was hard to take in, but in that moment there was a rise of hope, an expectation that I could again meet the mother who had given birth to me. The woman who I had thought of pretty much every day of my life. And here she was. The last time she had held my hand, I was a few days old. But now again, she could reach out to me, she could grasp my hand. She could hold me. And I could hold her.

Back home, I read every word. Again and again.

'To my darling daughter.'

'I don't know if this will ever reach you.'

'I want you to know that I love you.'

Christmas after Christmas. Birthday after birthday. Every one. She never missed the day.

There was even a photo of her and her children. It turns out I had two brothers and a sister.

The Call

The agency had explained that if I wanted to move forwards with meeting my birth mum, I could write a letter to her which they would send on. They would then forward any reply and from that we could arrange to meet up.

That's what is meant to happen. But I took a different route.

One item that the agency was able to give me was a copy of my original birth certificate. I had never seen this before and had assumed that with a closed adoption, it shouldn't exist. But it did. It appears that the agency's practice was to keep such things after all. And here it was.

Alongside my birth name and my birth mother's name, was the name of my father. It was an Asian name and the certificate gave details of where he worked. A taxi company in Birmingham.

Back home, and in full Sherlock Holmes mode, I searched for a phone number. Yes. The taxi firm still existed, and here was the number.

Nervously, I pressed the digits into my mobile.

'Hello, is it possible to speak to . . .'

'Yes, speaking.'

'Oh! Hello! This may sound very strange but my name is Selina and I'm an adopted child. For the first time today, I've been able to see my original birth certificate and it's your name. Can I ask . . . Is it you? Are you my father?'

'Hello, Selina. Of course I remember this. I'm a friend of your mum's. Actually, I'm not your father. That's somebody else. But your mother needed a name on the birth certificate and we're good friends, so I let her use mine.'

My hand is shaking, trying to hold the phone. My heart is racing. There are tears in my eyes. Could this really be happening? Could I actually find out where my birth mum lived? Could I meet her?

'We're still friends, Selina. If you like, I can call her and pass on your number.'

Within an hour, my mobile started to buzz. Swallowing hard, I picked it up.

'Hello?'

'Selina? It's me. It's your mum.'

McDonald's Car Park

We met that same evening. McDonald's car park next to Bescot Stadium, the home of Walsall Football Club.

Monica, my birth mum, lived in Erdington and drove up to meet me. I was too nervous to drive, so Eddie took me.

I saw the car drive up. I saw her get out. A tall woman, big boned, a little worn with the years but still identifiable—she had sent a photograph in one of the Christmas cards, so I knew what she looked like.

And there, in the middle of McDonald's car park, a mother and a daughter held each other. It was the start of something new.

We sat in the back of my car and talked. Not that long really. Just a bit less than an hour. During that time, I learnt that I had three younger siblings, the eldest of whom was currently in prison.

I learnt that Monica had struggled in giving me up for adoption. She had changed her mind on a few occasions before finally going ahead with it. She had only been eighteen years old and had no supportive relationships to help her.

And of course, Monica learnt about me too.

'You've got how many children?! And you're only twenty-one?!'

I remember at one moment, she looked at my arms.

'Selina! What are they?!'

My arms were bare and showed the many scars where I had self-harmed in earlier years. I explained. She became angry.

'But I gave you up for adoption so that this sort of thing would never happen! How can that be! I shouldn't have done it! I'm so sorry.'

Tears began to flow. Hers and mine.

As we drove away, I felt like a child again. Hope was rising. Something significant had just happened in my life. I had found the woman who'd given birth to me. The woman who had given me away. But she didn't hate me—she loved me.

The following months saw lots of interaction. I would visit Monica and spend time with my brothers and sister. They came over to Mum and Dad's house to celebrate Sophie's birthday. We would text pretty regularly and meet up when we could.

One of my first visits was to the young offenders' institute to meet my oldest brother, Dean. Dean and I got on particularly well. I guess we'd both had a tough time of it growing up and, in a sense, we could share the scars.

Crashing Down

It wasn't to last. Less than a year after meeting Monica, everything came crashing down. It was my sister's birthday as well as my own, and Monica had arranged for the two of us to celebrate together. Eddie and I went over, taking Eddie's two older children with us. I think he was upset that the party was really to do with my sister and less to do with me. Somewhere along the line, he began to argue with Dean and this escalated.

It ended up with Monica throwing us out of the house, telling me that if I wanted to come back, it would have to be without Eddie.

'You need to choose, Selina, it's me or Eddie. It's not going to work otherwise.'

I chose Eddie. We drove away.

Try Again

It would take a further six years before I got in contact with Monica again. By then, she had had my fourth sibling, a little boy.

Really it was my decision not to contact Monica for those six years. Eddie hated her. He was extremely jealous of me having any relationship with her and, of course, I was in the middle of that relationship with all the darkness and mind games that it entailed.

Mum and Dad weren't much better. They didn't like her much. Monica would swear a lot, chain smoke and make some pretty crude jokes, all of which were completely disgraceful to Mum and

Dad. Added to that, they started using Monica as an excuse for the reason we argued. It was just easier not to contact her anymore.

I kept in touch with Dean, though. And it was Dean that helped as a catalyst towards restoring the relationship. Not that Mum and Dad were particularly supportive of me getting in contact again. And Eddie, of course, was extremely angry.

We met a few times, but Monica and I had to admit that due to the stress of my relationship with Eddie and, to a lesser extent, the disagreements between Monica and Mum and Dad, it wasn't working.

I tried some counselling, helped by the adoption agency. This really did help me. I began to understand some of the pressures on an adopted child, some of my reactions as a kid which resulted from this. I read a couple of books, recommended by the counsellor, and these were a great help too. My sadness, though, was that Monica chose not to have any counselling herself. It seemed to me that all the attempts at keeping the relationship sweet were from my side, not hers. Inevitably, we started to drift.

It's not been easy since then. It's not been the easiest of relationships. There's lots of reasons. When we first started spending time together, we'd share the lyrics of Christina Perri's song, 'A Thousand Years'. Back then, it reflected a sense of hope and connection. As the lyrics say, we had found each other—and for a time, that meant something. While we were still in touch, there was one thing that Monica noticed:

'Selina, you're not well. I can tell. You're scared of your own shadow. The cannabis is controlling you and so is Eddie. I don't know what to do about that, but I can tell that these last few years have not been easy for you. You need to do something.'

Of course, I did eventually do something. Caught in an abusive relationship, on a cocktail of antidepressants and regularly using cannabis to manage my life, it was a dark time. And it's pretty clear that all of that together was a further cause for not being able to continue my relationship with Monica.

Chapter Nine

The Scrounger Shame of the Baby Machine

Yes, you read that correctly. The title that is. The scrounger shame of the baby machine. Headlines in a newspaper. Just when I thought things couldn't get worse...

Although it started so beautifully.

Magazines

Megan and Tegan had been born when I was still eighteen. They were premature and it was quite an event when they finally came home from the hospital. So much of an event, that it made the local newspaper.

It was a couple of years later, still in my early days with Eddie, when *Chat Magazine* called me. They had a copy of the newspaper article and wanted to write an item reflecting on the premature births, alongside the fact of them being children number four and five.

Move on another year, and there was a phone call from *Now Magazine*. They had a copy of the *Chat Magazine* article and wondered whether I would be willing to be part of a piece they were writing. They wanted to interview a number of young women who had never worked. There would be five of us altogether, all in our early twenties. One would be from a rich background, someone who had never needed to work. One would be happily 'kept' by her husband. Another would be disabled and another unemployed. I would be the fifth, having had so many children at such a young age, resulting in my need to stay home.

I said 'yes'.

All five of us went over to Birmingham for something of a fashion photo shoot. When the article appeared, it had been well written and sensitive to each of us and our different backgrounds. I enjoyed reading it and was grateful for the way it had been presented.

But it's what happened next that caused the problems.

Newspapers

Within a few days of the magazine being issued, I started to receive phone calls from newspapers. In the end, I agreed to participate in an article, written in *The Sun* newspaper. They were kind to me, and the article gave a good explanation as to how I had become a mother to six children by the age of twenty. Other newspapers followed, some contacting me but some writing without any communication at all. Journalists began to knock at the door, photographers hung around in the street. There were so many cars at one time, it blocked the whole road.

I did another agreed article for the Birmingham-based *Sunday Mercury*. Again, they wrote well, sympathetic to my journey.

Other newspapers were still approaching me, but I declined any more interviews. This didn't go down so well. It seems that if you turn down an interview with the *Daily Mail*, they will make up an article anyway. And having been declined, they were more than happy to write aggressively. The headline read:

> At just 20, this mother gave birth to her sixth child by two fathers. She claims £1,120 benefits a month and will soon be moving to a council house paid for by you. Regrets? Not one.

The majority of the article was then practically a copy of my agreed pieces with *The Sun* and the *Sunday Mercury*, but the damage was done with the headline.

The *Daily Express* followed a similar line. One of their photographers managed to catch me just outside the house. Wearing an old T-shirt and jeans and with hands in my pockets, it was a gift to complement their headline:

> Single Mother of Six . . . and she is aged just 20. But a free house and £1,120 a month is still not enough.

The *Daily Express* went on to comment that I was 'shamelessly negotiating to sell her story.' Translated, this meant that they were upset I had written a piece with *The Sun* rather than with them! And, again, what came across was incredibly negative.

The local *Express and Star* were no kinder, with an editorial saying somewhat sarcastically that the then Chancellor of the Exchequer, Gordon Brown, should just keep 'sending the cash.'

The worst was yet to come. The *News of the World*, at the time a Sunday sister paper to *The Sun*, approached Darren. The resulting piece was devastating. The headline said it all:

> *The Scrounger Shame of the Baby Machine.*

The subheading advised that my ex was going to reveal 'the shocking truth about the single mum.' And so he did. Darren was quoted:

> *Selina is a one-woman baby machine and wants everyone else to pay. She hasn't done a day's work in her life. All she wants to do is have kids and take the State's free cash. For her, another baby means another free handout. She sees them as her meal ticket.*

The newspaper painted Darren as the put-upon husband with me trying to persuade him to give up work because State benefits would pay a higher amount. The article suggested that I was forcing Darren into having more and more children. They made little mention of the fact that it was Darren that had walked out on our relationship.

With the various newspaper articles coming out, everyone wanted a piece of me. Hate mail started arriving on a daily basis, accusing me of scrounging off the government system. And they were the polite ones. I burnt the letters but can still recall the trauma of reading accusations and lies, along with so many swear words. I tried to laugh about it. But it hurt.

The follow-up letters page in *The Sun* was not as kind as the original article:

> I was shocked to read about a single mum having six children by the time she was 20. I wonder how many she will have by the time she is 40?
>
> Selina claims she spends a fortune on nappies, baby lotion and milk. Doesn't she mean that the State spends a fortune?
>
> What a pity she couldn't find the energy between pregnancies to nip along to the family planning clinic.
>
> She has obviously been taught no moral standards.
>
> If she wanted these kids, she should pay for them.

I felt shaken. I had unleashed a storm of malicious abuse.

Most of this happened over about six months in 2004. These were still comparatively early days for the internet, and I'm grateful for that. But even so, there were message board sites on the internet where people were discussing me and using words that I simply can't bring myself to say.

Radio stations got hold of the story as well and I was the subject of a number of dial-in chats. I happened to hear one of them on WM Radio, so I called myself and they allowed me to speak. That changed the debate slightly in my favour as the radio host commented that I didn't sound like a scrounger!

Further 'fame' was to follow, and I was asked to appear on *This Morning* on television with Fern Britton and Philip Schofield. They treated me well and my story was well presented. But again, there was a backlash. More hate mail. More abuse.

Offer of Help

The *Now Magazine* team were genuinely upset with what had happened and they contacted me to suggest a follow up article. This came out a couple of months later and was really helpful. The headline on their front cover said, 'I've got six kids but I'm no scrounger' and the article went on to explain that Darren had left me with no prior warning. It discussed my own adoption and pointed to a positive future for all of us.

What was even better was the fashion shoot that went along with the article, with all the children being dressed in clothes from Next, Monsoon and Marks & Spencer's—they looked so smart!

It was kind of *Now Magazine* to offer the help—and it did help. But the press were still asking for more, and the hate letters continued. It pushed me indoors. It was hard to walk out of the house with reporters hanging around and photographers looking for pictures that would support the prejudiced views of their newspaper.

Recluse

I chose the word carefully for this sub-heading. Recluse. That's exactly what I became. I was afraid to open the door, afraid that photographers would be on the doorstep.

This was about the same time that things were getting difficult with Eddie. His control of me was almost absolute, hence my difficulty in trying to leave the house anyway.

I became sick—head-to-toe psoriasis.

My reclusive behaviour also developed a compulsive behaviour. OCD stands for 'Obsessive Compulsive Disorder.' I became obsessed with cleaning the house. Everything had to be spotless. As soon as the kids were out of the way, I would start cleaning—every day in exactly the same way. All the floors would be vacuumed. Every corner of every room would be dusted from top to bottom. Every chair and table polished. Any ornament that had been touched by anyone would be wiped clean. I would meticulously go through the bathroom and kitchen, cleaning every single square inch. Nothing would ever be left with a speck of dust on it. Everything needed to gleam. Every day. Every single day.

I remember a friend of Eddie's coming round.

'Selina, what are you doing?'

'I'm cleaning of course!'

'But I was here yesterday. You were cleaning then! No one's been round since. There's nothing to do. Why are you doing this?'

The question was a good one. There was no need to clean. There was no reason to clean. But it became a compulsive behaviour. Something that I had to do every morning. A repetitive process. I felt I couldn't function unless I had cleaned the house first.

Even with the children, I had a particular routine that they were obliged to conform to. They each had to sit in a specific place to eat their breakfast. They were then all required to go upstairs and clean their teeth and were not allowed down until I had vacuumed the floors and removed every crumb.

Once the children had left for school, the kitchen would be dealt with. Even if I had cleaned it thoroughly just the day before, it would be done again. Every plate in its place, every bowl stacked precisely, every knife and fork meticulously placed in the cutlery drawer.

Process upon process. Repetitive, unnecessary, damaging. It got to the point where the OCD was controlling me. I could do nothing outside of the repetitiveness of cleaning and caring for the kids. There was nothing else. There could be nothing else.

I knew it wasn't right. I'd often find myself crying whilst I cleaned. Asking myself whether this really was the total sum of my life, whether there was any meaning at all, whether I should bother to continue to live in this way.

My awareness of having OCD, coupled with the treatment I was receiving from Eddie, meant that I was desperately unhappy. OCD was controlling me. Eddie was controlling me. I covered it up by smoking copious amounts of cannabis. But surely, I would ask, as I cleaned the vase for the fourth time, there *must* be more to life?

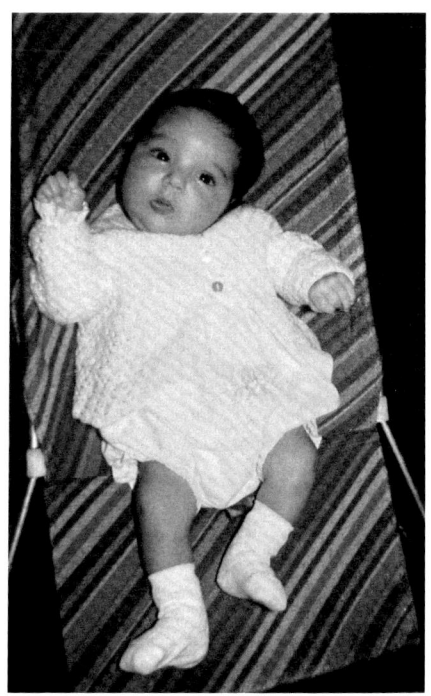

Seven and a half weeks after birth

Around five years old

My First Holy Communion, age seven

With my first child, Aisha, age 16

With Reece, my youngest of six, age 20

All six of my children

Newspaper article published in 2004

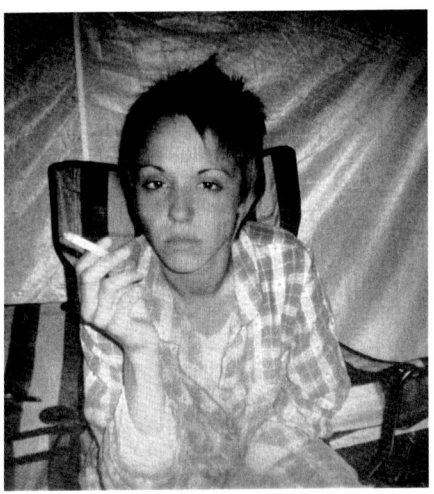

In my twenties

The wreckage of my car after my suicide attempt — 28 December 2015

First-year promotion from Charis Bible College — May 2017

Graduating from Charis Bible College — May 2018

Wedding day with Andrew and our grandson Kaiden — 20 August 2018

With Andrew celebrating my 40th birthday in Jerusalem, Israel — 2022

Receiving the keys to our building — Reboot Ministry & Keystone Church — January 2023

With Andrew and Andrew Wommack at
Grace & Faith — May 2023

Mission trip to Africa — August 2025

Chapter Ten

Breaking Point

I wasn't living, I was existing.

Eddie was out of my life by now, but I can't say things were much better at all. I was still experiencing full-on OCD, cleaning the house every day. I was still fearful of stepping outside. I had no idea what a normal life should look like, having been in bondage to Eddie for such a long time.

I would force myself to leave the house. Even if it was only to go shopping.

I had no idea what the future held, no concept as to what life should be like and little appetite to live it.

God had other ideas.

'Jesus Loves You'

It was a Sunday afternoon and, for once, I had managed to get out of the house with the kids. Most of them were in the car as I pulled up to the local mini market to get some milk. As I walked towards the shop, I saw Carl. A six-foot-tall black guy, quite a bit older than me, someone who clearly looked after his fitness levels. Carl was somebody I knew vaguely from my time in the church youth group with Clare. He recognised me before I recognised him.

'Hey, Selina, how are you?'

'Oh, I'm really well, thank you!'

It was clear I wasn't well at all. My cannabis habit had affected my sleep and my appetite. I looked so skinny, whatever I wore hung off me. There were bags under my eyes and I stared in an anxious manner at pretty much everybody.

As I left the shop, Carl was still there.

'Selina, I just want you to know, Jesus loves you!'

'Oh, thank you.'

'Would it be alright for me to take your number? Cora and I would love to stay in touch.'

We exchanged numbers. As I drove home, Carl's words stayed with me. Jesus loves me? Really?! Surely if he really loved me, my life wouldn't be in such a mess?

Conversations

Carl was persistent. He reached out to me on Facebook, regularly reminding me that Jesus loved me.

'Cora and I would love to meet you! How about we go for a walk at the Arboretum?'

And that's how my conversations with Carl and Cora became a regular event. It was mainly Carl that I met as Cora was working during the day. Carl had this kind of unofficial street ministry. As a Christian, he felt concerned for those he identified as being on the edges of society and I was certainly one of those.

My walks at the Arboretum and my conversations with Carl began to make me aware as to how crazy things had got.

'This is not normal, Selina. You're not living a normal life. Far from it. You're not leaving the house, you're afraid of everybody you meet. There's even a fear in your eyes. You don't have to live like this.'

Carl wasn't pushy with his faith, but the conversations were just so helpful for me to understand that there was a different kind of life I could live. I'd forgotten what normality was. The abuse I had received from Eddie had created somebody afraid of her own shadow.

As I reflected on those conversations with Carl, I began to recall the way I used to live. The fun I used to have with Clare. The trips to the pub. The days out.

Once upon a time, I'd had a life.

'Carl, I can see what you're saying. I need to change. I know I need to change! But it feels so dark. I feel in the darkest of places. My thoughts feel dark. Most of the time, I'm thinking about crazy stuff—death, suicide. I'm not sure whether I believe in the devil or not but, if he exists, he's most definitely in my head and in my house.'

Trying

Carl and Cora tried to help. They were genuinely encouraging. They invited me to church. But in my mind, to go to church I had to be a better person, I had to dress in smarter clothes. The problem was I had no smarter clothes. Eddie had been so controlling that I wasn't even allowed to wear skinny jeans, let alone any kind of fashionable dress.

I tried to change my behaviour. I tried to stop drinking Lucozade—I was on about five bottles a day at the time. I cut down on cigarettes. I gave up smoking cannabis. But things just got darker. I couldn't function. I had constant migraines, regular anxiety attacks. I was so anxious about my own body, that I felt unable to undress, unable to have a shower, fearful of the way I looked. It felt like the world was ending. No matter how hard I tried to come off cannabis, I'd always go back to the dealers, always back to the drug.

If it is possible, things got even worse at this point. Aisha was ill, the kids were out of control and Social Services were threatening to take them away. I stopped caring what I looked like. I stopped opening the curtains. I stopped getting dressed in the morning and would just hang around in my pyjamas.

Church in the Park

With my mind in the state it was, Carl and Cora were a real lifeline. Practically the only time I was getting out of the house was to visit them or to go walking in the Arboretum with Carl. I wasn't particularly interested in their Christian faith and, still being spaced out on cannabis, my mind wasn't really engaged anyway. But I appreciated their love and care. They didn't push their faith on me but would very gently ask how I was doing, whether they could pray for me, whether I would begin to believe in Jesus...

One Sunday afternoon, walking with Carl in the Arboretum, we began to approach what was clearly some kind of performance. In fact, it was a number of churches working together, presenting Jesus in the open air.

Carl smiled. 'Selina, haha, you won't go to church, but it looks like church has come to you!'

I wasn't really interested or engaged in what they were saying. That was until a lady came to the microphone and began to speak about her own story. She had been addicted to cannabis for many years but her new-found faith in Jesus had enabled her to completely change her life. It did seem to be a bit of a coincidence that I would be listening to this particular testimony as we walked past. Carl smiled again.

'Selina, let me introduce you.'

Her name was Fiona.

'Good to meet you, Selina. Hey, would you let me pray for you?'

'Sure.'

'Lord Jesus, I pray for my new friend. Would you meet her in her need? Help her overcome her addictions. Come close to her. Help her find you.'

I was shaking. I could hardly stand on my feet. I must have looked quite a sight. I was at my skinniest, little more than skin and bones with no clothes to fit. My eyes were deep in their sockets, my cheeks sallow, my hair short and spikey. I was fearful and it showed. But there was something about Fiona's prayer that piqued my interest.

'I'll let you get on your way, but I'd love to invite you over to our church,' Fiona said. 'We have a midweek meeting this coming Wednesday. How about you come along?'

I made all the right noises just to end the conversation, took her phone number and left with Carl.

The Meeting

Back home I felt more desperate than usual. It seemed to me that the prayer had made me worse. But there was something stuck in my brain about going to Fiona's church meeting. Eventually I gave in to the prompting, called Fiona and on that Wednesday night went along to her church.

Fiona is white but married to a black man and their church was a typical black Pentecostal place. I really didn't know what to make of it all. As far as I was concerned it was all a bit happy-clappy. I don't recall much of that first time at church and certainly nothing stuck in terms of what was preached.

One thing I do remember is pulling over into a lay-by on the way home from that meeting and phoning Carl. He worked nights for a mental health foundation.

'You'll never guess where I've just been. I went to church with Fiona!'

'Oh wow! That's wonderful! How did you get on?'

'It was okay, I think. I'm not quite sure what to make of it but I thought you'd like to know that I went along.'

'Absolutely! I'll be praying for you!'

Into Darkness

I'm not sure Carl's prayers worked. Having been to church, I tried once again to come off cannabis. But the results were not good. It was like I was falling into darkness. My mind felt totally scrambled, my body was physically shaking.

Social services had been involved in keeping an eye on the kids, but I remember that their concern at this time switched to me. They persuaded me to go to a counsellor but even that was no use. In the end the counsellor admitted he was unable to help.

I was back to hanging around in my pyjamas, keeping the curtains shut, unable to help even with the children. One time I drove out to the countryside, to Milford Common, on the edge of Cannock Chase, still wearing my pyjamas. I spent most of the day sleeping in the back of the car. I have no real idea why I did it. I could have slept at home. But I just wanted to be out, away from everything, away from me.

I really didn't care. I remember getting out of the car and walking into a pub to use the toilets. I got more than a few glances, with my hair a complete mess, still wearing my pyjamas.

I tried to stay off cannabis. I really did. The doctor prescribed some antidepressants, and they helped a little. But it wasn't long before I was driving over to the dealer.

Another Me

The strangest thing was happening every time I smoked cannabis. I felt guilty. I felt convicted that I was following a course which was simply no good for me or my family. It was like there was another me. One part of me just didn't care and was desperate for the next smoke. The other part was shouting for me to give up, to try again, to be better.

Talking to Carl on the phone about it, he once again invited me to church. This time I went.

There was a guest speaker who brought some kind of prophetic word for me. I didn't really understand it all, nor him, but the word itself, on reflection, carried a lot of sense. The man said to me that he saw I was in a lot of darkness and thus I was desperately unhappy. But then he saw a light and that there would be a happiness that would find me.

I noticed something else that morning as well. Whilst I was in the church meeting, I didn't feel anxious. My anxieties seemed to disappear. I felt a peace, a renewed confidence in my ability to deal with the pressures I was facing.

So I went again. And again.

I started to take some of the children. I tried to pray. I tried reading the Bible one day—there was a bit there about those doing evil not coming to the light. I shut it again quickly!

It was all a bit hit and miss, not helped by some of the congregation who insisted that I really shouldn't wear ripped jeans and should stop smoking cigarettes. Some of the people there were really lovely and genuinely cared for me. But there was also a lot of religion. I don't ever remember hearing a clear gospel message that God loved me and that Jesus could change my life. It was more about trying to change yourself, doing the right things. All very legalistic.

Despite my experience at church, I couldn't quit smoking weed. In fact, if anything, it got worse. I couldn't sleep. I didn't really want to sleep. When I did, I began having vivid dreams. I'd wake up frightened, feeling there was a presence in the room. What was happening? Why was this happening? I comforted myself with another smoke.

Desperation

I felt schizophrenic. One part of me didn't care, the other part desperately wanted to change.

I decided, once again, to give up cannabis.

It was a disaster. I felt a complete wreck. I even seemed to be losing my short-term memory as a result. Constant migraines and constant anxiety overwhelmed me. But I kept on, trying to do my best, praying that God would come to the rescue.

'If you're there, God, please help! I can't do this. I'm trying, but it's not working.'

Chapter Eleven

The Vodka and the Knife

Trying to please God. That was pretty much my concept of Christianity at the time. I had no real relationship with Jesus and genuinely felt that if I could improve my life, then I'd be able to find God. But if my life stayed in the mess it was, then there was no way God would want to find me.

Things came to a head over Christmas that year. I'd stayed off cannabis but that made Christmas Day extremely stressful. I was trying to give the kids the best time I knew how, trying to please everybody, visiting Mum and Dad, being the best I could be.

The whole thing led to extreme anxiety, and a desperation to get back on the weed. I needed to get to church. The problem was, there was no church over that Christmas break and on the first Sunday when we were due to meet, church was cancelled.

That place of peace, that sense of peace that I felt when I entered the church building had been taken away from me. I didn't know what to do.

The migraines continued. The anxiety was intense. The two voices in my head were shouting at each other. It all became too much.

Suicide

I remember the day. 28th December. That's when things came to a head. I woke feeling extremely depressed, not knowing what to do, not really wanting to do anything. I took myself down to the kitchen and there, on the table, was the bottle of vodka that Dad had bought me for Christmas. I wasn't that much of a drinker—much more into my drugs. But this seemed to be a way out.

I started to drink, tipping back glass after glass of neat vodka. By the time I was more than half way through, there was a knock on the door. It was Carl. He was so angry with what he saw and poured the rest of the bottle down the sink.

'What are you doing, Selina? What on earth are you doing? The kids are upstairs! Shame on you!'

And with that, he left.

It just made me angrier. Condemnation piled on top of depression. The kids could see that by now I was pretty paralytic. They all left the house and went round to Mum and Dad's.

A few minutes later, Dad was at the door.

'Why are you doing this, Selina? Stop it! Why are you acting this way?'

We started to argue. I was shouting at him, full volume. I made a lurch for the car keys. Dad got there first.

'Give me those car keys, Dad! Give me them now! You have no right to stop me. You can't tell me what to do. You're not my real dad anyway!'

It was the last comment that pushed him over the edge. He flung the keys at me and walked out of the door, slamming it behind him.

There's a motorway bridge less than a minute from my house. I decided to end it all.

Calling my birth mum, I told her what I was going to do. I walked out of the house, car keys in hand. Reversing out of the parking space, I swerved into the street and slammed my foot onto the accelerator.

I didn't make it to the motorway bridge. I didn't make it to the end of the street. I was so drunk, I couldn't steer the car. Near the end of the street, driving at around fifty miles an hour, I smashed into a parked car.

The crash was deafening. A metal-twisting, glass-shattering moment. And then—silence. A hollow, suffocating silence.

I was still alive.

A wave of despair hit me harder than the impact itself. This wasn't supposed to happen. I wasn't supposed to be alive.

Pathetic. I couldn't even get this right.

Half a bottle of Smirnoff burning in my veins, I had climbed behind the wheel, determined that today would be my last. The motorway bridge was waiting. One sharp turn, one final moment, and it would all be over.

But instead, here I was, broken, bleeding. But breathing. My head had smashed through the windscreen, my legs tangled in the wreckage of the dashboard. Fifty miles an hour. No seatbelt. And yet, against all odds, I had survived.

Despite the impact, I was able to get out of the car and even search for my cigarettes.

By now, the street was beginning to fill. The daughter of the car owner came out of the house, screaming at me.

'That's my dad's car! He could have been in it! You crazy woman!'

Neighbours were screaming and shouting at me. Asking me, what did I think I was doing? Monica, my birth mum, arrived, and then Sophie. Not long after, Dad was on the scene, with most of my children. Dad and Monica began to argue, screaming and shouting at each other.

The police and the fire brigade came. I remember a policeman leaning over and whispering to me as he stared at Dad and Monica, saying, 'No wonder you wanted to kill yourself with that kind of family!'

'I'm so sorry, officer, it's my fault. I've been drinking. There was no one else involved.'

Perhaps it was because of Dad and Monica almost fighting in the street that the police were so sympathetic. They drove me around for a while in order to get my alcohol levels lower before taking me to the police station. They allowed me to stand outside the station to smoke a cigarette. But in the end, I was arrested and for the rest of the night remained in a police cell.

The Vodka and the Knife

In a strange way, I felt that God was with me that night. I started praying the Lord's Prayer over and over. It was practically the only prayer I knew to pray anyway. I repeated it again and again, hour after hour that night. I felt God's peace.

As I sobered up, I began to feel an intense disappointment with myself. I was angry, but not at God, not at others. I was angry with me. How could I possibly get into this state? What had I become?

I was released pending further charges, and I asked the police to drop me off at Carl and Cora's house.

'I'm so sorry. Please forgive me. I've been so stupid.'

They prayed with me and for me.

That same day, I called round on the man whose car I had destroyed. He was kind enough to say that he wasn't concerned about the car but about me.

I was banned from driving for eighteen months.

I felt vulnerable, still on edge, unsure what to do next. I didn't feel in control anymore. I was scared to smoke or drink, unsure I could control my behaviour.

The Knife

Most of the time, I felt like I was in some kind of dream, not really in the real world.

There was a knife in the kitchen. It had a serrated edge. I felt drawn to it. I held it in my hand, running my thumb up and down the sharp edge.

I hadn't self-harmed since my teenage years, but that morning there were deep cuts on my arms and wrists.

There were voices in my head. One voice was screaming at me to kill myself. The other was telling me that I could do better.

I was still going to church. Whenever I heard a particular Bible verse that had some resonance for me, I'd write it out on a post-it note and stick it to the bedroom wall.

Fight the good fight of the faith.

For the weapons of our warfare are not of the flesh but have divine power to destroy strongholds.

Take up the shield of faith, with which you can extinguish all the flaming darts of the evil one.

We are more than conquerors through Him who loved us.

God gave us a spirit not of fear but of power and love and self-control.

Be sober-minded; be watchful. Your adversary the devil prowls around like a roaring lion, seeking someone to devour.

You get the idea. It shows where my mind was at for sure. Scriptures about fighting and survival rather than verses showing God's love and peace. It wasn't long before the wall was covered with Bible verses. My kids thought I'd gone mad. Maybe I had.

The sadness was that I still didn't have a Christian faith. I was treating the Bible verses as self-help verses, believing that I could fight and win this battle myself.

It showed itself in other ways as well. Constant church attendance to pretty much every meeting. Occasionally reading the Bible, but still not understanding it.

Random God

I didn't know God, but God knew me.

One day, when it was all feeling a bit too much, I went back to the drug dealers. I could see the look on their faces. They were almost leering at me. They knew I was back, they knew I was hooked, they knew they had me.

With cannabis in my pocket, I walked away and in a random moment decided to call in at Walsall College. Looking through the different courses listed, I wondered whether I should enrol. Still pondering this, I walked on as far as the Arboretum.

It was while I was walking around the Arboretum that the most bizarre thing happened. A couple in their forties approached me and asked me whether I had ever thought of further education. It turned out that they were commencing some courses at Walsall College and were giving out leaflets.

'Well, that's pretty amazing. Have you been following me? Would you believe I have just been at the college, looking through the courses?'

'Ha! That must be the big man in the sky looking down on you!'

The man wasn't a Christian but those were the words he chose.

'We run stand-alone courses at the college. We're teaching GCSE level English and Maths. You should come! We meet on Mondays and Fridays during the week.'

My immediate reaction was panic. I was still entirely OCD-driven. Monday was the day when I needed to spend at least ten hours cleaning the house, following on from the kids having been there over the weekend. And Friday was my preparation day for the kids. Again, I needed to clean the house. How could I possibly go to college?

Having reached home, I pulled the packet of cannabis out of my pocket. Opening the window, I threw it out.

The following Monday, I walked through the doors of Walsall College.

A House of Darkness

Things were improving. But not really.

I was a different person when I was at church or at college. But the moment I walked through the door back home, the clouds descended. The house just felt dark to me. I almost found a comfort in the darkness. I turned back to the fearful, anxious person that I felt I had always been. I felt depression fall on me like a cloak.

I sat in my bedroom, looking at the scriptures I had posted on the wall. As I stared at John 3:16, 'God so loved the world that He gave his only son', I saw an enormous spider. I have a bit of a phobia about spiders, so I was genuinely frightened. This was a big one and it covered the whole of the scripture. I looked away, not sure what to do. When I looked back, it was gone. There is no way it could have disappeared within the split second of me looking away and looking back.

I'm certain there was a demonic presence in that place. I saw some red eyes staring at me one time, and really, it didn't freak me out at all. I felt almost a comfort from it. Something that I was used to. I felt and saw things often.

And then, the moment I left the house to go to church or college, the feelings would shift. There would be a brightness about me, an awareness of what was happening around me, a desire to live.

Baptism Before Salvation

I was still going to the same church, and they announced they were having baptisms and invited me to take part. The problem was, no one had actually explained the gospel. No one had told me that Jesus loved me and that I should invite Him into my life. So I was still struggling on, trying to be the best me I could. And with that in mind, I agreed to be baptised.

Despite me not having a living faith, I do remember a very clear hand of God upon me, particularly through one song which I would play again and again. It's by CeCe Winans and is called 'Mercy Said No'. It tells of sin trying to get hold of me, but mercy says 'no'. It speaks of God's sacrifice being sufficient. I played it over and over during those days before my baptism. Even though I would say I had no living faith, I was holding onto the words of that song, almost in desperation. I might think that I was caught up in drugs, anxiety and depression. But mercy said 'no'.

My big hope was that baptism would change everything. As I walked to the venue, the song continued to play on my headphones. I needed mercy. I wanted forgiveness. But there was so much conflict within. I had no clear understanding of salvation. And as I came out of the swimming pool that the church had hired, all I felt was rather wet. I felt no different. Where was this God? Where was this change that everyone had promised? If I felt any difference at all, it was a feeling of disappointment. Worse than that, there was a feeling of loss, of increased darkness.

'God, I'm not really sure what's going on. Nothing has changed—I still feel the same. I'm not going to give up though. I can't. Mercy says no and so do I. Please help me, God.' The battle was well and truly on. The week after my baptism, every dark and anxious thought came back. I was constantly thinking about suicide. I felt completely spaced out—pretty much how I had felt from the moment I came out of the swimming pool. It felt dark, truly dark. I regularly stared at the serrated knife.

Darker Still

It wasn't just me struggling. The children were having dreams at this time as well. Dreams of me being in a battle, dreams of me running off into darkness.

I bumped into Eddie in the town centre. He offered me a joint. I took one puff and gave it him back.

I felt so shaken by what was happening. All the old pressures were back. I ended up phoning Eddie and asking him to come round and bring drugs with him. I sat outside in his car, smoking cannabis. Eddie spoke:

'You'll never be any different. You'll never change. You'll always be like this. Drugs have got you. You will always be controlled.' For a few moments it felt like I had come back under Eddie's control. But the control was not really Eddie of course.

I don't suppose he really knew what he was saying, though looking back, I know exactly where those words were coming from. There was a battle for my soul. And if I was going to fight that battle myself, I was going to lose.

The next two weeks after seeing Eddie, I smoked more cannabis than I had at any time in my life. The lowest, darkest, weirdest, craziest two weeks of my life.

Eddie started calling me again, constantly texting me, wanting to meet up. In the end I had to stop it and report him.

I don't remember sleeping. I'm not sure what I did. I was in a constant cannabis haze. I went over to the library at one point and took out a number of haphazard books on Christianity. Walking over to the Arboretum, I would read them for hours on end, in between smoking yet more cannabis. My head felt like it was exploding. Nothing seemed real. I was trying to hold on to my sanity by playing 'Mercy Said No,' again and again.

Chapter Twelve

Random Facebook

I was quickly slipping into a totally hedonistic lifestyle. Meeting up with my blood brother, Dean, we went out clubbing. I was smoking weed and drinking far too much alcohol. There was a strange man in my bed, one morning. He didn't stay long—one look at the Bible verses on the bedroom wall led to a swift exit.

And I was still considering my own exit. If I couldn't beat smoking cannabis, what was the use? If baptism didn't help, what could? If God wasn't there, why bother?

I was still constantly playing 'Mercy Says No.' Without it, I'm not sure I'd be alive today. The lyrics kept telling me that although I deserved justice, I could receive mercy.

I struggled to make it to church the day after the bender with Dean. I had no transport of course, having lost my driving licence. But I got there regardless. I remember holding on to the seat in front of me through the worship. My body was shaking. My head was a mix of prescriptive drugs and a hangover. I hadn't slept in what seemed like weeks. I hadn't eaten properly in what seemed like months. Something had to give.

Sheepishly, I went over to talk to the pastor after the meeting.

Strange Advice

I told the pastor everything. All that had happened over the last few months, all that I'd done the night before out on the town. My complete addiction to cannabis. My fears and anxieties. The darkness I felt in the house.

'Come back on Wednesday night and we will pray with you. We'll sort out some deliverance.'

Somehow I stumbled home, still a complete wreck, now trying to hold out for this important Wednesday night encounter.

That Wednesday evening, the pastor was there with his wife, along with one or two other leaders, including Carl. For about one and a half hours, they shouted and screamed at the top of their voices.

'Devil, come out of her! Demons be gone! I command you to go in Jesus' name!'

It didn't seem to have any impact. If anything, I felt worse. I felt a darkness around me.

'Out of her in Jesus' name!'

I remember feeling an intense darkness settle over me at that moment and a feeling of being controlled. They would raise my arms and tell me to keep them up but I would continually say no and lower them.

I remember replying, 'I'm not coming out. She's mine.'

And with that, I felt an increased darkness coupled with an irrational fear.

Really, that was it. Around one and a half hours of being shouted at. And I wasn't any better afterwards. Maybe just a little deafer.

Leaving that meeting, I felt completely drained. My body felt as if it had been run over by a bus. And there was such a darkness, a presence that I had never really known before so acutely. It was pressing in on me. My mind was buzzing. As I travelled home, I was caught by yet another migraine and a complete sense of hopelessness. Coming out of that meeting, my desire to smoke and to harm myself was stronger than it was when I had gone in.

I had been told to come back the week after for a second session. I was wondering whether I'd be alive to see it.

Help Me!

By the time I got back home, the kids were in bed. The pastor's wife phoned me. I ignored the call. Carl's wife Cora called me. I ignored the call.

Sitting down in the lounge, I picked up a pen and paper. Reflecting on what I had just gone through, still shaking at the thought of it, I began to write:

> *In my dreams I have felt like I belong to a dark presence and today that dark presence was in me. It controls me and I belong to it. When I stood up, I was shaking and sweating so*

badly and when they tried to touch me, I wanted to pull away. I nearly shouted at them 'no!' My insides were fired up and it was like a storm had started. So many demons were fighting but there was one who was stronger and more powerful and that one was in control. I have never felt such a spiritual force at work in my body. I'm so confused and torn about where my loyalties lie. If Jesus loves me, I pray he delivers me. I am full of evil, and it is very scary.

I pulled the coffee table towards my sofa. Taking my Bible, I opened it randomly in front of me. Walking into the kitchen, I fetched the knife with the serrated edge and placed it next to the Bible. I still had some cannabis and rolled up a joint, placing it on the other side.

Sitting back on the sofa I looked down at the three items. There were voices in my head telling me to pick up the knife. Silencing them as much as I could, I shouted out a simple prayer.

'God, help me! God, help me!' I screamed. 'God, what am I to do? How am I to choose? Please help me!'

It was all I could say. I felt numb, almost in a trance. My head was screaming 'it has to end, it has to end!'

At one point, I picked up the knife and found I was still holding it some hours later when I awoke. Quietly, I crept up the stairs so as not to wake the children, taking the three items with me.

The knife and the joint were tucked inside the pages of the Bible, next to my bed, for the next four nights.

It was on the second or third night, still with the three items next to my bed, that I decided to write God a letter. I've kept it and here it is:

Okay, God. I think I've had it now. I'm scared to surrender my all, because I've never been my all. I don't know what my all is. I've always repressed a part of me and never felt whole, so how do I surrender my all when I don't know what it is?

Please help me to find me. It's easy to think with my head that I've surrendered to you, but I haven't, have I? I don't know where to begin. All the hurt and the constant hiding. I've never been touched in my heart completely. Never felt overwhelming love; it's always conditional. So how do I surrender to you? Numbness has always been my friend, always kept me safe, kept that locked up part of me whole. I give myself to something but not my all. There's always something holding back.

I don't know what real feelings are. What is love? How can you love me when my own mother couldn't? When people try to love me, I hurt them to stop them getting close. It's like the real me can't be loved, only the fake me. But the fake me is only going to get fake love back. Please help me.

I had cried to God for help. I didn't know it just yet, but He had listened.

Grace and Faith

The next morning, feeling no better, I decided to text an old friend. You may remember Steph. She's the Christian friend that used to live in Leicester and had been part of that early youth group. By now she was married and living in Cheltenham, but we had stayed in touch.

I had seen a random Facebook post from Steph about a conference. That's what reminded me about her.

My text was a fairly simple one.

'Steph, I'm in a mess and I don't know what to do.'

She replied almost straight away.

'You need to pray.'

What a stupid answer, I thought. How was I supposed to pray? What was I supposed to say?

'Okay, God, this is me. I'm praying like Steph said. I need your help, God.'

Almost immediately, a scripture reference came to mind. I don't know how and I don't remember reading this scripture previously. It's from Isaiah chapter 31 and this is what it says:

> *Woe to those who go down to Egypt for help and rely on horses, who trust in chariots because they are many, and in horsemen because they are very strong, but do not look to the Holy One of Israel or consult the Lord!*

I sent another text to Steph, explaining what had happened. I was confused but Steph was excited.

'This is amazing! This is God telling you to listen to him and to ignore any other voices.'

'Steph, I think I need to do something about this though. You know that conference that you were advertising on Facebook, are you going?'

'No, I can't go. You should though.'

So I did.

The conference was the very next day. I took a train to Telford and walked into the Grace and Faith conference, organised by Andrew Wommack Ministries.

And I can't say it did me any good. I sat and listened, but walking out, I felt pretty much the same. I took a train back to Birmingham and called in at my usual church. They were holding an all-night prayer meeting. It felt like they were talking more to the devil than God and it made my heart pound and my head hurt. I lasted an hour or so before I left.

As I walked back to catch a bus, I saw people falling out of the pubs and enjoying themselves in the nightclubs.

'God, I don't understand. I don't know where I belong. I don't belong in the pubs and nightclubs anymore. But I don't feel that I belong in church either. God, I still don't know what to do.'

Chapter Thirteen

Darkness to Light

The conference hadn't been particularly great for me but I decided to go back again the next evening, anyway.

I hadn't managed much sleep, only arriving home at 7 am. I slept on the landing for an hour, afraid that if I actually went to bed, I'd not wake up in time to go back. Something was bugging me about needing to get back to the conference.

Autopilot

That morning, I'm on autopilot.

Collect the kids from Mum and Dad. Take them to a party. Sort out my travel.

And all the time, feeling so extremely anxious. If this God thing didn't work, what else was there? My emotions are all over the place. Turning my gaze to my bedside table, I see the Bible enclosed around the knife and the joint. Which was it to be?

Quite honestly, the knife seemed to me to be the best option.

Having taken the kids to their party, and then dropping them back to my parents, I call the Pastor's wife.

'I'm going to a church thing today. I hope it works. It has to work. Something has to happen. If nothing changes, I really am going to end it all. Today will be my last day.'

By now, I'm running late. Really late. It's early afternoon and I realise the conference is about to start. When things go wrong, they can go wrong big time. Maybe it was the enemy's activity, aware of the way that I was trying to change my life once and for all.

As I run down the street towards Mum and Dad's house, I realise I've left my phone behind. Back to the house, mobile safely collected, I press the button to call Dad for a lift. No signal. Bizarrely, the phone had decided to reboot itself and it was taking forever.

No use phoning Dad then, and not worth taking the risk that he would be in anyway. I make it to the bus stop, realising that I only have ten minutes before the train leaves for Birmingham. That was a problem as even if the bus arrived immediately, the journey to the station is around fifteen minutes.

A sermon pops into my head. A visiting African pastor had spoken at church about asking God to take control of his time. So I do the same.

'Please God, slow down that train. If you want me to make this conference, you need to slow that train down. Make it late. Help me catch it.'

Eventually, I get to the station. The train is still there. I get to Birmingham.

'Well, thank you, God. It seems you are interested in me after all.'

But as I arrive on the Birmingham New Street platform for the Telford train, I see that it's empty.

'Excuse me, is this the right platform for the 14.11?'

'I'm sorry, dear, you've just missed it.'

It is another half hour before the next train. But at least that allows me to try and sort my phone out. It had finished rebooting now, but the battery is dead. A kind person in a phone shop allows me to recharge for a few minutes, so by the time I get back for the next train, my mobile is working.

It is as I'm literally stepping onto the train that I receive a call from Monica, my birth mother.

'It's Dean, your brother. He's had a stroke.'

What to do? One leg on the train and one still on the platform, it's a real dilemma. I decide to text Dean and push on.

Now on the train to Telford, my problems don't finish there. I've taken a book out of the library, all to do with the Tabernacle. It is quite a hard read to be honest and it was one of those random books I had picked off the shelf just because I identified it as being vaguely Christian. To be honest, I don't understand much of it, but I keep reading. And before I know it, I have gone past my stop at Telford.

Getting off the train at Oakengates, the next stop on the line, I don't know what to do.

I see a group of people walking out of the station and I run to catch up.

'Excuse me, can you help me? I'm meant to be at a conference in Telford, but I've missed my stop. Do you know how far Telford is from here?'

'What do you want to go to Telford for? Some kind of boring conference? Why not come with us —we're going to a beer festival. That's much more fun!'

To this day, I've no real idea as to what time I eventually managed to get to the Grace and Faith Conference. But I did arrive, although still in something of a daze. The combination of a frantic journey along with a largely sleepless night meant that I wasn't really with it. It was not helped by my need to smoke a joint before I went into the meeting!

Not Wanting to Live

I must look a sight. At least two people come up to me and offer to pray with me. This is a bit of a novelty, but I accept their prayers anyway.

There is still some time before the next session in the main hall and I find myself at the bookstall.

'Hello, can I help you? Are you okay? You don't look too well.'

'Well, yes, I don't really want to be here.'

'So why have you come?'

'No, I don't mean not wanting to be at the conference. I don't want to be here at all. I don't want to live!'

She asks my name.

'Selina, my name is Jane. Right now, you need the Holy Spirit. So go into the conference and come back and tell me what happens.'

That seems downright odd. Tell her what happens about what? What did you think I was going to do, Jane? I've just fought a mighty battle to be here. Of course I'll go in to the talks. But it is just a talk from some kind of pastor, after all, isn't it?

I give her a quizzical look, promise I'll come back to her and walk into the auditorium.

Words of Life

Andrew Wommack is speaking at this session. I sit down, trying to join in with the worship, most of the time wondering how people can get so excited about a song. Or so it seemed to me. The talk itself is well underway before I begin to realise that for the first time, I can understand what is being said.

It's not that I didn't understand previous preachers at my own church, but this is different. The words are getting through. It is like a light has been switched on in my brain and for the first time I am understanding whole passages of scripture that have simply been words before.

As Andrew speaks, I begin to realise that God really does love me. That no matter what I've done, His love for me is constant and unchanging. He's always loved me, and always will do. I begin to shake in my seat, holding on to the seat in front of me.

This is real! God *is* real!

There is revelation after revelation, as I listen to Andrew. For the whole of my life, I've been speaking negatively. I had spoken death over myself. I had declared that I didn't want to live, that it would be better to die. My words over my own life had been words of death.

'God, I get it! I understand! I need you! I want you in my life!'

Revelation after revelation rolls over me. How have I missed this? How had I not understood that God had sent his own son Jesus just for me? That he had died and would have died even if I had been the only person alive? Unconditional love. That love flows over me as I sit in my seat, quietly shaking, for the first time aware of God in a way that I hadn't thought possible.

The Prayer

At the end of his talk, Andrew invites anyone to the front who wants to be baptised in the Holy Spirit. I'm thinking that this is what Jane has talked about at the bookstall. That this is what I must need.

I walk to the front.

'Actually, before we pray today, I just want to check one thing. This is a Christian conference but there may be people here who have yet to encounter Jesus Christ. If that's you, I'd like to lead you in a prayer and introduce you to your Lord and Saviour. If there is anyone here who doesn't know Jesus, please put up your hand.'

My hand is up in an instant. This is it. This is the truth. This is what I need.

There are as many as three hundred people at the front of the meeting, but only two of us have raised our hands for salvation. With my hand still in the air, I pray a prayer that changes my life.

> *Father, I'm sorry for my sin.*
> *I believe Jesus has already paid for my sin and I receive that forgiveness.*
> *Jesus, I make You my Lord.*
> *I believe that You are alive, that You now live in me.*
> *That I am saved, I am forgiven.*
> *In the name of Jesus,*
> *Amen.*

As I open my eyes and lower my hand, I hear Him.

'You belong to Me now.'

Words of love. Words of affirmation. Words I never knew I needed so deeply. For the first time in my life, I belong. I belong to Him. I know it. The doubts have gone. Fear has evaporated. All those years of feeling like an outsider, unwanted, unloved—they've melted away in this moment... I am held in His arms. I can feel His love, steady and overwhelming. I belong to Him now.

Andrew is speaking again.

'We're going to receive the Holy Spirit now. All those of you at the front are going to be baptised in the Holy Spirit. The Bible tells us that one of the first signs of being full of the Holy Spirit is speaking in tongues, just like the disciples did at that very first Pentecost. And that's what's going to happen today. As I pray for you, raise your hands in the air and expect that the Holy Spirit is going to come upon you. He will fill you. And you will speak in tongues.'

I have no doubt whatsoever now, that God is going to meet me in this way. Having shown me in such a powerful way how much He loves me, I know for sure He is going to fill me with His Spirit.

As Andrew prays, I feel an intense presence within me. At that moment, I'm not sure exactly what it is but now I know that He, the Holy Spirit, had come upon me and filled me.

There is a rise of worship within me. It feels like I want to shout for all I'm worth. Out of my mouth comes a stream of words that I don't know, that I don't understand. Worship, worship, more worship.

As I walk back to my seat, there is an overwhelming feeling of joy. This is a high beyond any high I have ever experienced. It doesn't compare with drugs. It is more intense than cannabis, more powerful than alcohol. I don't feel like I'm in the room. I'm in the heavenlies. I'm with Jesus. I know Him. And He knows me.

I Don't Want This to Go

At the end of the meeting, I join a prayer line.

'What is it you would like prayer for?,' Alan asks.

'I want to keep this. This feeling. I don't want it to go away, ever.'

Having explained to Alan that I had been one of the two people to raise a hand, he prays for me and introduces me to Lucy. I didn't know it then, but Lucy is to become a close friend. We exchange details and I exit out of the auditorium, still in a daze but, oh, such a different daze compared to the drug haze that I was used to.

I walk over to the bookstall. I don't have to say anything. Jane can see straight away what has happened. She is so excited. I get to take any five books from the stall, free of charge.

On the train home, I can't contain my excitement. I am telling everyone in the carriage what has happened to me.

'Jesus is real! Jesus is real! He has changed my life tonight. He can do the same for you!'

I guess with me, there are no half measures!

It was a complete revelation! In a moment of time, I had become a completely different person. The old me had gone completely and been replaced with the me that God created me to be. Paul, writing to the church in Galatia, writes, 'I have been crucified with Christ. It is no longer I who live, but Christ who lives in me' (Galatians 2:20). And that was it! I no longer had to be the person that I had been. I could step over into this brand-new identity and be someone completely different. It was almost as though I saw the old me die in front of me—kind of like when you see in a movie, someone turning into pixels and disappearing. And left in their place is a brand-new creation.

The Bible tells us that 'at one time [we] were darkness, but now [we] are light in the Lord' (Ephesians 5:8). If ever there was a verse that applied to me that evening, it was that one. I had stepped over from darkness to light. I had gone from being completely dead to completely alive. All in one night.

Chapter Fourteen

Identity Change

'God, I hope you don't mind me saying this, but I'm not satisfied. I want more.'

My conversation with God continued throughout a long walk from Walsall railway station, back to my house, having missed the last bus. But in a way, I appreciated the walk. Time to talk with God. Time to think through what had happened that evening. Time to say thank you.

I got back to the house at about 2.30 in the morning but didn't go to bed. I took out my hidden stash of cannabis, I gathered together all my prescription drugs, and opening the bedroom window, I threw them into the garden, shouting at the same time, 'I am healed by the blood of Jesus!'

I'm not sure I was a particular blessing to my neighbours at that point in the morning, but it had to be done. And it was done. For me this was a complete healing, a complete release from my drug-controlled behaviour. I was different, I was clean. And I intended to stay that way.

Recording the Change

I didn't sleep at all that night. I *couldn't* sleep that night! My mind was buzzing. There had been so much revelation as to who God was and what He had done for me, all in one evening. It was hard to take in, but not hard to understand. I couldn't stop thanking God.

That night I wrote a letter. Every other word in it is a thank you to God. I couldn't stop praising him. I couldn't stop thanking him. I was free from addiction. I was free from self-harm. No more thoughts of suicide. Free from anxiety. I found the letter recently. This is what it said:

> *At the altar it was me and God. I told him 'I am ready, Lord. I am yours.' I am blessed! God is good! I am a child of God! At that altar I experienced oneness with Christ for the first time. I realised that I had been denying Him His place. It was me, not Him. I love God, Jesus and the Holy Spirit. I spoke in tongues all the way home. I am no longer addicted. I have decided that I am not an addict anymore. Now I live for Jesus, to glorify His holy name properly. God is so good. At the beginning I wanted to die but at the end I had eternal life. I listened, I acted, and I spoke. Jesus answered. All I wanted was to be filled with the Holy Spirit and now I am! God's grace is amazing. He got me through the last two days in amazing ways. I have been touched by God, and I'm not satisfied! I am hungry, so hungry, and I want more of God, much more. I want to overflow with His love. I am delivered. He has set me free—the truth has set me free. I will hold on to this blessing. Nothing will take it away. My God is awesome,*

priceless. He is magnificent. I need no other. He is my Father. God, I love you!

What I started that night became a pattern over the next few months. I would write everything down. Every thought about God, every insight from reading the Bible, every dream I had, every reflection on listening to a sermon. It all went into my journal. A journal of thanks.

The next day was Sunday and before heading back to the conference, I went to church. But, of course, I was so different, and everyone could see it. For me, my eyes were suddenly opened to the kind of meeting I had been attending. The worship wasn't the same when compared to what I had experienced at the conference. And I was suddenly aware that during the whole time I'd been at that church, they had never actually preached the gospel.

Charis

By that afternoon, I was back at the conference. I wandered around the atrium before the next session and noticed a stand that I hadn't seen previously. There was a banner above with the word 'Charis'.

'So what is Charis?'

'We're a Bible college. We're based in Walsall.'

'You're based *where*? Walsall?!'

'That's right.'

I'd never noticed the college in all the time I had lived in and around Walsall. But there it was—just around the corner from where I used to buy my drugs.

'My name's Antoinette. And here's a pack for you. It explains everything about Charis and what the college does. Take it home, have a read through and see what you think.'

Ten minutes later I was back.

'Here you go!'

'What's this?'

'The completed application form. I'd like to sign up please.'

'But you've only just received it. Don't you want time to think about it?'

'No. I'm absolutely certain that this is what I need to do.'

And there I was, one day after becoming a Christian, signing up for a Bible college! But God was in this. I knew He was. Reflecting now, He had prepared me for this moment. Even the people that I met on those first two days at the conference—so many of them have become good friends.

Fern was behind me in the queue for the auditorium. We are close friends to this day. Jane on the bookstall. Antoinette on the Charis College stall. Lucy, who prayed for me at that first meeting. Shirley and Ali who befriended me. Charlie and Jill who were leading worship that weekend. John who was overseeing the meetings. All of them, today, are good friends. God not only prepared my heart for that transformational moment, but He prepared a good bunch of friends to help carry me through in my new-found faith.

Reboot

God did another thing that day. I found that He was giving me different ways to express my faith, and a real boldness to do so.

One of my first conversations was with my daughter, Tegan.

'It's like this, Tegan, imagine that God has created a virtual world. You know, something like The Sims game. He made this world, and he made Adam and Eve. And he was communicating with them—He was sending them text messages, and they were replying.

'God would text them. He'd say, "how are you today?" And they'd reply, "We're awesome. This is such a beautiful place you've made, God. Thank you. Thank you for what you've done."

'But then one day, God sent a text message and it didn't get through. It was blocked. A message came back saying, "Error, virus detected."

'So, Tegan, that was when sin entered the world. But God had the answer. He had the antivirus. His name was Jesus. And He sent the antivirus to the world. When you install the antivirus into your operating system, your system gets rebooted. So, if you ask Jesus into your life, you get a complete reboot. He gets rid of the old software, and you get brand new software. That's the new life that Jesus gives you.'

I didn't know it then, but that first discussion with Tegan and the way I explained the gospel became much more for me in the weeks and months to come. The whole concept of getting a reboot was one that would stay with me.

Family Faith

It wasn't long after talking to Tegan that she chose to give her own life to Jesus Christ. Her twin sister, Megan, also prayed with me and two ladies from church, asking Jesus to change her. Within a few months, Aisha had prayed the same prayer.

A short while afterwards, I was back at my home church and had been asked to share my story. I did so. I shared practically everything. Every crazy moment, wrong turn, wrong relationship … I laid it all out, and then spoke of that glorious moment when Andrew Wommack led me in a prayer.

I mentioned earlier that this church, to my knowledge, had never had a gospel call. But today they did. It was really in response to what I shared. At the end of the meeting, for the first time in all the months that I had been there, they invited people to respond to Jesus. Two of the first to stand at the front were my own daughter and son, Sophie and Reece. It was hard to stop the tears that night.

Just prior to the meeting, Sophie had assured me that she had absolutely no interest in becoming a Christian and that she was only attending the meeting because I was speaking.

God did the rest.

Hungry

I was so hungry for more. I wanted to be at every meeting. I couldn't stop reading the Bible. I was praying all the time, wherever I was.

Identity Change

Within a week or two of becoming a Christian, I was travelling round to every local church I could find that preached Jesus Christ. Walsall Community Church, All Nations Church in Wolverhampton, many more . . . I was just so hungry, I wanted to hear every bit of wisdom that I possibly could.

My enthusiasm went well beyond the walls of any church building. I found myself witnessing in Walsall town centre alongside a lady called Sue, from Wales. I signed up to abseil down a building in order to raise money for mission, despite being afraid of heights. And again, for charity, I jumped from a plane. The funny thing is, I had only flown in an aeroplane for the first time two weeks before jumping out of one!

All of this coincided with me completing my college course. So, alongside joining Charis College, I was now the proud owner of educational certificates with qualifications in Maths, English and Business Studies.

Although I had the privilege of seeing a number of my children give their lives to Christ, it wasn't all positive in the family. Monica, my birth mum, wasn't in the least bit interested. I had kind of assumed that my adopted mum and dad *would* show more interest, but nothing could be further from the truth.

Dad kindly gave me a lift to my interview for Charis College.

'What do you want to be doing this for? It's a waste of time! Why are you going so hard at this? Everything has to be black or white for you, doesn't it?'

In that last comment, he was correct. If this was true, if Jesus Christ really was the way, the truth and the life, then I absolutely was going to go for it. Nothing was going to stop me. This was life changing. No more cannabis. No more prescription drugs. No more counselling. No more negative talk over my life. I was healed and set free. I'd had an identity change. I was rebooted.

Yes, I was an adopted daughter. But I was adopted by the King of Kings and Lord of Lords.

Chapter Fifteen

The Drummer with the Smile

My radical lifestyle had not yet affected my smoking. Sure enough, some well-meaning friends at Charis were concerned for my ongoing habit and promised to pray for me. To be honest, I felt a bit annoyed. My whole life had been transformed in the last couple of months, so why should smoking be such a big issue?

A God Intervention

There was one very definite upside to continuing to smoke, and her name was Tanya. One day, I was out in the Arboretum with Carl, along with some of my kids. I took some time out from playing ball games in order to have a smoke and it was then that I met Tanya. In fact, we wouldn't have met, had she not asked me for a light. It was the start of a friendship and two months later, I had the real thrill of seeing her come to Christ and find her own living faith. Tanya went on to study at Charis as well.

There was a visiting speaker at All Nations Church in Wolverhampton called Todd White. I had not heard of him, but I later found out he's quite well known. During his talk, he began to speak about giving up habits and being set free.

In the ministry that followed, some of the team were walking through the congregation and praying for different individuals. A lady approached me and began to pray. The next thing I remember is being on the floor. I'm not sure how I got there. I'd seen people fall over under the power of the Holy Spirit on a number of occasions by now, but I hadn't been somebody who had particularly responded in that way. In fact, to be honest, I had avoided falling to the floor and resisted any physical pressure to do so. But this time, it was different, and there I was, pulling myself up.

No sooner had I got to my feet than another member of the team came along and prayed again. Again I hit the floor. Again, I got up, only for a third member of the team to pray. This time, I decided to stay lying down! This didn't stop another team member praying for me yet again. I was shaking under an overwhelming presence of the Holy Spirit. At one point, I actually begged the woman to stop praying for me. I could hardly stand up for over an hour afterwards.

One of the common themes within all four sets of prayers from different team members was that of freedom and deliverance. It was interesting that they each chose to centre on that, as the majority of prayer in ministry that evening was for a Holy Spirit fire to fall, in line with Todd's talk.

Despite all this ministry and because I had been set free from so much, I didn't really apply Todd White's talk to my smoking, and did not relate to the fact that each team member has specifically been praying for deliverance and freedom. But that night, back home, I heard God speak to me so clearly.

'Selina, you can give up smoking now if you want to.'

To be honest though, I still didn't want to give up. My instant reply to God's prompt was exactly that! I didn't want to give up. And I was still smoking the next morning.

Back at the conference, I went out for a walk with my friend Tanya, during a break in the morning seminars. I'd been smoking for over twenty years and had never been accosted by anybody for throwing my cigarette butt on the floor. But that morning, the moment I threw it down, a man approached me, telling me he was a local enforcement officer and would be fining me for littering the pavement. I didn't take it well, but back at the conference, I began to realise that God was making a point.

I asked my new friend Tanya to take the cigarette packet out of my pocket without me wanting to even touch it, and I asked her to throw it in the bin. She did. And from that moment on, I have been free from any smoking addiction and have never had a desire to smoke again. I remember it was July 2016. Exactly two months since God had met me and changed me. And now He had dealt with my remaining addiction in a rather dramatic way. I have honestly never craved a cigarette since that moment.

I was so hungry to learn more about the Bible, it became my new addiction—but the best kind of addiction ever! I was so eager to worship, I was visiting as many church meetings as I could. I found what was at least a temporary home at All Nations Church, Wolverhampton. To my delight, the four younger children were coming with me and were genuinely enjoying the meetings. The three girls – Sophie, Tegan and Megan – would sometimes hang around after the meetings along with other youngsters and take part in impromptu worship sessions. To see my children responding to the gospel was such a delight.

A Different Kind of Cleaning

God had cleaned me up, big time. But it wasn't just me being cleaned up on the inside that God was about.

God had dealt with my various addictions, and I was free from drugs and from smoking. There was one further problem to be dealt with, though. I was still cleaning the house, pretty much every day, top to bottom. But something began to change here as well. My OCD in cleaning had very much related to a sense of depression and a lack of purpose in the past. But as I continued to clean, I began to realise that any sense of depression had completely lifted.

Most days, at that time, I was still getting up at 5 am and after showering, I'd prepare breakfast for the kids. Once they were out of the house, I would then dust downstairs, wipe down the kitchen surfaces and then vacuum the whole house.

The OCD has gradually disappeared over time. There wasn't a dramatic moment when I suddenly threw down the duster and discarded the washing up gloves but, over time, things have changed. I do still like a clean and tidy house but I no longer panic if I don't have time to clean it every single day!

To The Rescue

Having been a student at the course at Walsall College, I had begun to study a little, but was still nervous about signing on at Charis in terms of the study required. That first morning, arriving at the college, receiving my welcome pack and meeting other students was something of a trial. Everyone there had obviously been Christians for quite a time and here I was, three months or so into my new-found faith. Everyone seemed to want to hug you and all I wanted to do was tell them to get off me! These Christians were just plain weird! They were all smiles and hugs and 'bless you's'. It was such a different atmosphere to practically anything I'd ever faced before. But one thing was clear, God had saved me, and God had called me to be here, so I'd put up with the hugs and get on with the course.

During one of the breaks, I sat with Lucy, sipping a coffee.

'Selina, can I introduce you to Andrew? You may have seen him in the worship team—he's our drummer. He's on the course with you, although he's doing the night school.'

This good-looking man, half English, half Jamaican, with the biggest smile, shook my hand.

'Good to meet you, Selina, it's going to be a fun year.'

Lucy went on to tell both of us about a friend of hers called Patrick. Patrick was struggling with drugs and had threatened suicide. Because of my similar background, Lucy asked me to pray for him. The problem was I had no idea how to pray! The only thing that came into my head was 'In the name of the Father, the Son and the Holy Spirit!' I resisted praying that particular prayer, but the panic was showing on my face.

Seeing what was happening, Andrew jumped in and prayed for Patrick. I had been rescued.

Unbeknown to me, Andrew had already spotted me, not just as a new student but someone who he might like to get to know!

Later on in the week, Andrew saw me in the café.

'Hi, Selina, how are you?'

'I'm alright thanks, apart from I've got this really painful neck today. I don't know why.'

'Oh, that's great!'

'Didn't you hear what I said?! What do you mean that's great? I'm in pain!'

'I know. And it's great because God's going to heal it. Let me pray for you.'

He did, and the pain went. Instantly.

I started bumping into Andrew at the local shops. He lived nearby, but I can honestly say that I'd never met him or remember meeting him locally until after we were introduced at Charis. Looking back now, I think these local meetings were something of a God set-up!

With a conference coming up at the college, Andrew offered to give me a lift each day as I was still not able to drive. We were just friends but perhaps there was already an undercurrent of something more.

The Chestnut Tree

'Selina, I've got some news. I'm moving back to London to work and to be nearer to my children. I'm going to have to finish year one through the correspondence course.'

'Oh, that's a pity. I'll be sorry to see you go.' Everyone seemed a bit 'spiritual' at Charis and Andrew appeared a bit more 'normal'. I would miss that.

Andrew did still come up to Charis on occasion though, to play the drums in meetings or to visit friends there. It was on one of these visits that a meal had been arranged by mutual friends at the local carvery, The Chestnut Tree. Andrew picked me up but upon arriving, there was no one to be found. Everyone else had cancelled.

We chatted over the meal, and I was telling him of a number of Charis friends who had called round at the house.

'You invited them in, but you never invited me in? Why is that?'

'Because I could never find anything wrong with you.'

Andrew leant back in his seat and looked at me quizzically.

'I thought you didn't want any friend-friends?'

'That's right. I don't want any friend-friends.'

But despite my assertion, we were both beginning to think that there may be something more to this relationship. No words had been spoken, no promises made—yet there was a shift. Gentle and unmistakable. It was the beginning. The beginning of something beautiful.

The texts began to flow. Then it was phone calls.

A couple of weeks later, Andrew called round. We were on our way to a mutual friend's party. He was a bit early and we sat rather awkwardly at opposite ends of my living room. Suddenly, he stood up, walked towards me and knelt in front of me.

With a smile on his face, he said 'Are you going to kiss me or what?'

Over the next few months, Andrew would come up on occasion and together we would go to meetings and call on friends, without actually telling anyone that we were now an item. I do remember telling the children though.

'So, who's Andrew?' Megan asked one day.

'Oh! I know who he is!' said Sophie, 'He's the drummer with the smile!'

Chapter Sixteen

Reboot

I remember when it was. Andrew had moved back from London and was living locally. It's September 2017, and we're sat in Nando's. And I'm wishing that I wasn't quite so honest with God!

'What are you thinking, Selina?'

'What do you mean?'

'I'm serious. What are you thinking?'

'Oh, nothing in particular.'

'I don't believe you.'

'Well if you're so sure, why don't you ask the Holy Spirit to tell you?'

So he did. Andrew's smile broadened, if that were possible.

'God's just told me. He says that you're wishing I would hurry up and ask you to marry me.'

I stayed silent but couldn't hide the smile. And that's when I'm wishing I'm not quite so obvious towards Andrew and in what I talk to God about!

Andrew didn't ask me then, but it wasn't long before he was kneeling in front of me at our engagement party with all our friends cheering us on.

Together, we completed year two at Charis Bible College, and we married in August 2018.

Different

Perhaps we've always wanted to be different, and this was reflected in our choice of venue for our wedding reception. Fazeley Studios in Digbeth, Birmingham is well known for its urban art, and most of our wedding photos have a background of modern graffiti. Maybe we were influenced by those early missions together in Germany. Let me explain…

It was two years before our wedding and we weren't even dating when an opportunity came up for mission. This was somewhat different to the kind of mission Charis students generally went on. It was to a Goth music festival in Leipzig, Germany.

Jeff Serio leads an organisation called European Initiative. He had been a visiting speaker at Charis and as a result, had invited students to join him as part of an evangelistic team at the festival. At that point in time, I hadn't travelled much outside of the UK and didn't know what to expect. Upon arriving, Jeff took us to one side to explain. Not that we needed the explanation—standing outside the gates of the festival, just observing the people going past, was eye opening.

Aside from the main stage, where the death-metal bands would play, the festival itself was split into different areas, including what was called a 'satanic park'. There was a 'fetish park' as well as a Goth market, including stalls with people demonstrating how to cast spells and put people into bondage. The bookstall included many books that were actually banned, because of the depictions of some of the worst forms of abuse. One book boldly announced that it would help you to get to hell. Witches were walking about, casting spells. Another section invited people to bathe in a pool, naked. The person with the tarot cards was definitely at the mild end of what we faced that day.

People were walking past, pretty much naked. I remember Andrew simply not knowing where to look! Some seemingly had tattoos on top of their tattoos! The body art was extreme, often depicting satanic rituals, screaming devils and some pretty weird looking creatures. Other visitors decorated themselves in chains, reflective perhaps of their mental state.

This was to be our mission field for the week. And a regular mission for the next three years. During that time, I spoke to satanists, witches and to so many more heavily in bondage to the devil. I met people who followed the practice of scarification, where they would carve pictures into their flesh using a knife.

It was so hard to break through. So hard to see anyone respond—they were lost in the personas that they had created and the life they had chosen to live. Many were clearly demon possessed and most refused to listen to any talk about God.

During my three years there, I only led one girl to Christ—she was a steam punk and not so caught up in some of the demonic that showed itself at that festival. I asked her if she had ever experienced real love.

'Not the kind of love at this festival. Not sexual love. Not just friendship. Real love. That's the love that Jesus shows you.'

'Really? You mean that's possible?'

'Yes, it's more than possible. You can ask God to change your life here and now. And you can know that same love.'

Right there, she began to cry.

'I would so like to have that kind of love.'

It was a privilege to pray with her.

Actually, many people allowed us to pray with them. Their openness to spiritual issues, albeit the wrong kind of spirits, meant that some were happy for us to pray God's blessing on their lives.

One time, I prayed for a young man who declared himself to be a satanist. He had an upside down cross tattooed on his chest. And as I spoke to him about God's love, he broke down in tears.

Some conversations were more surreal. There was one gentleman, dressed head to toe in metal and chains, who insisted that he wasn't human but was actually a tank.

That girl who gave her life to Christ was the exception. But we spoke about life. We declared the truth. And we trust that many of those conversations planted seeds that God, through the Holy Spirit, will water and bring to life.

Perhaps our Goth festival experience helps you to understand how we ended up with a graffiti-prominent wedding!

Honeymoon

It truly was a beautiful day. My two boys walked me down the aisle, my four girls stood beside me as bridesmaids, and at the end of it all, Andrew became my husband. It was everything I had dreamt of and more. We went to Croatia for our honeymoon. How we got there is a bit of a miracle. We only just had enough money for the wedding, but I was determined to have a real honeymoon and loved the idea of flying to Croatia. I found the ideal hotel on an island just off the coast, though it wasn't exactly affordable!

Somehow we gathered enough money for the airfare but quite honestly didn't have anything for the hotel itself. We prayed, trusted God, and decided to go anyway.

When we arrived and settled into our hotel apartment, we began to open the wedding cards that had been given to us. We hadn't had time to look at them before. And then, as we opened the first card, something incredible happened. Money started to spill out from the envelopes—more than enough to cover the hotel, more than enough to make our honeymoon unforgettable. We knew that God had provided for us, in the most miraculous way, blessing us beyond what we could have hoped for.

Speak Things as Though They Are

Our experiences in Germany, alongside the people we were encountering on the streets, often at the edges of society, lost to the system and lost to the life God intended, caused us to seriously consider our own ministry.

'Do you think that's alright, Andrew? I feel a bit of a fraud saying that we have a ministry when we don't.'

'But the Bible says that God calls into existence the things that do not exist. We need to speak things as though they are. Let's start to declare that God has given us a ministry. We know that He has, and we know that He's going to make it work!' And that's what we began to do. When we spoke to other Christians, we would say that we had our own ministry and as we stepped out in faith, God began to meet us for the task ahead.

We needed a name though.

Reboot Ministry

'What do you think to this?'

Andrew was holding a business card in his hand which proudly declared that the two of us were working as Reboot Ministry.

'It looks great. This is so exciting!'

We decided to call ourselves Reboot, based on the gospel explanation that I felt God had revealed to me. Andrew was using it as well and we found it very effective, simply explaining that everyone's system had crashed, that there was a virus on the software and only God could reboot us.

As we began to distribute the cards and engage people in conversations, the invitations started to arrive. Would we speak at this event? Could we preach at this church's evening service? Could we take a team to work with a group of churches?

By now we were in our third year at Charis. Year three is a leadership programme and everything we were learning went hand in hand with our intentions for Reboot. Every time we were challenged to write a mission statement and develop a vision; we used Reboot as the template. Reboot was to be missional and evangelistic. We intended to gather teams and to send them around the UK, throughout Europe, and even further. We wanted to invite teams to the UK. We wanted to train people. We wanted to be out on the streets.

That final year at Charis was essential. God really laid a foundation for what we were to do next. By the end of it, we had found a Christian graphic designer who helped us design our logo. We had jackets made with the logo on the back, ready for the teams that we would be working with.

We started working in local prisons as well. On one trip into Dovegate Prison, near Uttoxeter, we were accompanied by three older ladies. For an hour or so we spoke to five men and only later heard that each of them was a murderer and were being held on a psychiatric ward. Perhaps it was as well that we didn't know this in advance! Andrew and I told our stories and had the privilege of leading three of them to Christ.

On the Streets

As we stepped out in faith, others began to join us. We started regular outreaches in city centres and quickly found numbers of people who were ready to receive Jesus Christ and change their lives.

One of the things we had learnt from Jeff Serio and European Initiative was with regard to street drama. They had developed some excellent dramas, and we found these to be very effective in gathering a crowd in order to preach the gospel.

What started as a handful of people in the centre of Walsall on a Saturday morning, quickly grew to a larger number reaching out to various cities. There was such a hunger amongst those we spoke to. They didn't always pray a salvation prayer, but we had genuine conversations, touching on deep issues in their lives. Most times, they would allow us to pray for them and to ask God to bless them.

We quickly found that if we were willing to take a step of faith, God would meet us and provide. Consequently, as Andrew and I finished our third year at Charis, we decided to invite an American team to join us, working for a week in the summer. Twenty-four people arrived from the States! They were all part of European Initiative but were happy to work under the banner of Reboot Ministry. We found a mission house in Bloxwich to provide accommodation for the week, and planned numerous city centre outreaches in Walsall, Birmingham and Wolverhampton. In addition, we took them into the prisons. All twenty-four of them!

And that's how we have continued. We have continued to organise outreach events in various towns and city centres during weekends and holidays. We've taken a team back to the Goth festival, but this time as part of Reboot Ministry. Teams have travelled through the UK and beyond. Over the last year or two in the UK we have taken teams to Leeds, Bristol, Bath, Cheltenham, Gloucester, Derby, Nottingham, Liverpool, Manchester, Oxford, and up into

Scotland. Some of those teams were over thirty people strong, other times there has been just half a dozen of us. In partnership with European Initiative, we've taken teams to Paris, Lyon, Lisbon, Berlin and many more European cities. We've organised missions in Romania, Spain, Greece, Zimbabwe and on three occasions, Uganda.

Over the last three years, we've witnessed over 2,000 salvations! More than 700 people have been baptised in the Holy Spirit. Well over 100 people have been healed on the streets. And we've seen many prodigals come home to their Father God.

At the heart of everything we do is a passion for people and a deep commitment to helping them grow in their relationship with God. As a ministry, we pour in biblical values such as leadership, commitment, and team building—essential parts of living out our faith in community.

Our mission is clear: to teach the Word of God in a way that transforms lives. We focus on powerful, foundational truths— identity in Christ, righteousness, and what it truly means to walk with God. These aren't just lessons; they're the building blocks of a thriving spiritual life.

Like any journey, ours has seen people come and go. But over time, God has helped us build an incredible core team— seven people who carry the same heart and vision. As needs arise, we grow the team to meet the moment, especially during key events and evangelistic outreaches.

Personally, I know what it means to be completely lost—my life before Jesus was chaos. But now, He leads every step. I'm all in.

Whatever it takes to see people saved, to see our nation—and the nations—turn back to Jesus, I'll do it. Because this isn't just about ministry. It's about people, purpose, and a love that changes everything.

Chapter Seventeen

Family

Just because you are a Christian, it doesn't mean that you are suddenly free from the problems of life. Faith doesn't cancel out challenges—it gives us the strength to face them differently.

By God's grace, I overcame my addictions. But that was just one part of the journey. The truth is, I've still had to walk through tests and trials, especially in the area of family. It's been real, raw, and at times incredibly hard. But through it all, God has remained faithful.

The difference now? I'm not facing it alone.

Kaiden

Sophie had found herself a boyfriend, and not long after, we received the unexpected news that at just sixteen, she was expecting her first baby. It was a shock for us all. But then again, who am I to talk?

Kaiden was born with a chromosome abnormality called DiGeorge Syndrome. This condition can cause a range of health issues, including heart disease, cleft palate (which Kaiden had at birth), and potential learning difficulties. One of the most concerning issues was that Kaiden wasn't gaining weight, despite Sophie's best efforts to feed him.

Due to his weight problems and low immune system, Kaiden was in and out of the hospital almost weekly. It was a stressful time, but Sophie was doing her best to care for him and make sure he received the treatment he needed.

Then, on the morning of the 30th of April 2019, Reece's 16th birthday, we received a call from Jane, the lady who Sophie was staying with.

'Selina, you need to come over immediately. Something's happened.'

I could hear the distress in Jane's voice, but she wouldn't say anything more over the phone.

Andrew and I dressed quickly and left the kids with my parents, rushing to Jane's house. We didn't speak a word on the drive there, our hearts heavy with concern. We focused on God's word and His promises, not allowing ourselves to think the worst.

When we arrived, we were met with flashing blue lights: a police car, an ambulance, and a paramedic vehicle. My heart sank as I rushed inside, barely able to process what was happening. There was blue police tape blocking the stairs, and when I entered the lounge, I saw Sophie standing there, weeping uncontrollably, her head in her hands.

Jane approached me, her face pale, and pulled me into an embrace as she whispered the devastating news.

'I'm afraid Kaiden passed away in the night.'

Andrew and I were devastated, but we asked if we could see Kaiden. The police hesitated, and we didn't fully understand why.

A policewoman then escorted Sophie to the hospital, and we followed behind. When we arrived, we were led into a small side room while Kaiden's body was taken behind a curtain. We desperately wanted to pray over him, believing that even in that moment, God could restore his life.

'We need to see him,' I pleaded, 'Why won't you let us?'

The police officer was firm. 'I'm sorry, but we can't allow you to see him right now. I think it would be better if you waited in this room.'

We waited, along with Sophie, heartbroken and anxious.

Finally, the door opened, and two officers entered the room.

'You won't be able to see him until after an autopsy has taken place later this week,' the officer explained. The words hit us like a ton of bricks, and it felt as though time stood still. Our hearts ached with the need to say goodbye, but we had to wait.

Still in shock, our minds were racing with questions, not knowing what the next moment would bring. The whole situation felt like something out of a nightmare, but we kept moving forwards, trusting God to guide us through the storm.

Demonic

That night, back home, I slept with Sophie. I lay next to her and prayed over her as she slept, trying to bring her comfort in the midst of the overwhelming pain.

It was during the night that I felt a presence in the room. I'm not the kind of person to look for evil around every corner, but there was a definite presence that I couldn't ignore. I opened my eyes and saw it—like a shadow, but more than that. It was a spirit of death, standing over Sophie. I knew it was trying to attach itself to her, to bring more torment.

The atmosphere in the room seemed to thicken. I felt the weight of demonic spirits filling the space. I knew I had to take authority over them in Jesus' name. I reached for the bedside light, but it wouldn't turn on. It was strange, because it had been fine earlier that evening. I quickly grabbed my phone and turned on the torch. As the light filled the room, I declared Jesus as Lord over the situation. In that moment, the room emptied and peace returned. I continued praying for Sophie, commanding any presence of the enemy to leave, and declaring that Jesus would have the final say in this, just as He had on the cross.

It was sixteen months after he died before we were able to bury Kaiden, and almost three and a half years before the investigation into his death was closed, the cause of his death listed as natural causes.

Thankfully, Sophie found support in her new partner, Kyle. He stood by her through a difficult season, helping her regain some stability. Around three years after Kaiden's death, their daughter Nevaeh was born. Her arrival marked a turning point. With her lively personality and sweet nature, she brought a new sense of hope to the family.

There's something incredibly special about Nevaeh that has helped ease some of the pain. Her energy and joy have been a quiet reminder that even after deep loss, life can move forward. Nevaeh's presence became a source of joy and comfort, her infectious smile slowly mending broken hearts. Sophie and Kyle haven't had an easy path, but they've found strength in each other and continued to build their family.

Not a day goes by when I don't think about Kaiden and what it will be like to see him again in Heaven. I thank God that we got to have him with us for that short time. He will always be forever perfect in my eyes.

Mum

A little while before Kaiden was born, Mum was diagnosed with breast cancer. Thankfully, the treatment went well, and she made a full recovery.

It was a shock, therefore, when we heard that she had now been diagnosed with leukaemia. We weren't ready for that kind of news.

The treatment was intense and, while we were holding on to hope, it was clear Mum was struggling. She was losing weight fast, and the signs were there—she just didn't look like herself anymore. Sadly, Mum died on Easter Saturday 2020, less than a year after Kaiden's death.

All the family were able to be at her bedside and I know she had a genuine faith. She didn't take well to my expression of my own Christian faith, and I don't think we were as close as we could have been in those final years. But she was my mum. She had been a constant in my life and taught me more about unconditional love than I realised at the time. And I'm so grateful that all those years ago, she and Dad chose me.

I wish that Mum had lived to see me now. I know that our relationship would have been restored to what God would have intended, given the opportunity. I miss her, but I know I will see her again.

Children

Every family has its challenges, and ours is no different. But as I look back, I can't help but feel overwhelmed with gratitude. Each of my six children has been a joy—truly. They've all come so far, and they continue to grow in ways that make me proud beyond words.

Right now, Aisha has just finished her first year at Charis Bible College, and watching her transformation has been beautiful. Not long ago, her faith was more of a label than a lifestyle, but everything changed during a trip Andrew and I took with her to an Andrew Wommack conference in Colorado. Whilst there, someone prayed with her, and something shifted. She came home, got herself a Bible, and asked if she could join Charis. That was a defining moment for her.

Arun is navigating fatherhood and life while working at a casino. He has a six-year-old son, Che, who comes to church every Sunday—he's such a joy to be around and he brings such light with him. Arun's journey hasn't been easy, but I believe with all my heart that God's hand is on him, and I continue to pray that the fullness of His plan unfolds in Arun's life.

Sophie went through a deep valley after losing Kaiden. But in time, she found her strength again, returned to college, and is now a stay-at-home mum to Nevaeh. She and her partner Kyle just moved into a new home, and we see a lot of Nevaeh. She's a bright, happy little girl, full of laughter, with a spark that reminds me so much of both her mum and me.

Megan became a police officer at just eighteen. Independent, determined, and strong willed, she's bought her own home and has worked with at-risk teens, amongst other jobs. Tegan, her twin sister, is living in Spain, serving with Jeff Serio and European Initiative. She graduated from year three at Charis before she left and is now married to Samuel. Together they are serving God and seeing amazing results.

Reece worked alongside Megan for a while, helping those same challenging young people. He now works in telecommunications. He has learnt a lot from my mistakes, and is determined to do things differently!

I'm deeply aware of God's grace over my children's lives. We've been through a lot and, no, their childhood wasn't perfect. But each of them has fought through in their own way, and I have a strong, loving relationship with every one of them. I continue to pray that they will fully step into the life God has planned for them. I know those plans are good.

God has been so faithful. My children are such a blessing, and so is Andrew. I have a husband who is generous and caring—someone who puts me first. When I look back at the disastrous relationships in my past, all I can do is say, 'Thank You, God. Thank You for Your unfailing love.'

Chapter Eighteen

Keystone

At 8.30 pm on 23rd March 2020, Prime Minister Boris Johnson announced a stay-at-home order, effective immediately. Covid had well and truly reached the UK.

It was a strange time for everyone. We had to stop our Reboot activities, but we were aware of numbers who worked with us who still wanted to meet up. So, within the limits set out by the Government, we planned to do so.

No Churches

Up until this time, Andrew and I had been attending a church in Wolverhampton, with occasional visits to one in Walsall. The problem we faced was that these churches were choosing not to reopen, even though restrictions were not so restrictive as to require complete closure.

We wanted to meet. We had friends who wanted to meet, some of whom would benefit from that sort of contact, rather than try and stay on their own.

'What should we do? I can't find a decent church that has got its doors open!'

'Why don't we start to meet ourselves?' said Andrew. 'You know, just with our friends. We don't need to advertise anything, but at least we can meet.'

And so it was that we began to hire a hall at Emmanuel Church, a local Anglican building, from October 2020. Various lockdowns and partial lockdowns followed, but we kept meeting as and when we could.

If we were not allowed to meet in a building because of Covid, we'd meet outside in a local wood. We'd worship together, play games together—football and rounders were our favourites.

When meeting in a building was allowed, we would begin to gather at about 2 pm on a Sunday afternoon, on a fortnightly basis, with a service from about 4.30 pm. All we had was a microphone and a street speaker, with a few chairs in a semicircle. But it worked. And it grew.

We did life together. Bible studies in people's homes on a Wednesday night. Reboot missions in the week and on Saturdays. Church on Sundays. We'd meet up in Sutton Park to go walking together, picnicking together. We became friends.

The Call

By September 2022, we'd grown to about thirty people. Andrew had been feeling for a while that we were genuinely called to start a church, and that it should be called Keystone.

'I think we've got to launch properly, Selina. I feel God is telling me we have to go for this.'

'Are you sure? There's no way that I want to be just a pastor's wife! I'm not into coffee mornings, I'm not sure about just doing women's ministry.'

'Selina, you were never meant to just be the pastor's wife and I'd never want to limit who you are or what God's called you to do. Honestly, I don't believe this would hold you back at all. This is a journey we're meant to take together.

'We're not walking away from Reboot. We're not stopping the outreaches. But maybe now . . . we start being more intentional about caring for the people walking this path with us. We can do this, Selina. Together.'

And so we began.

We shared the vision with our core team and started to plan a proper launch for Keystone Church. At the same time, we were looking for another venue, one with more flexibility in terms of its use.

It was at one of our meetings in September 2022 when I felt God speak clearly about a future building. I shared it publicly.

'I feel God is saying that we're going to have our own building. And I believe that we will have it by January next year.'

It was a bold statement. I really hoped that I had heard God correctly!

Premises

We started looking for premises straight away. Old shop fronts and disused warehouses. But nothing seemed suitable.

I approached one of the church leaders in Walsall to ask whether I could use the pastoral WhatsApp group—a group of pastors in Walsall on the same WhatsApp—in order to ask whether anyone knew of a building. He advised me not to, but I wasn't entirely sure as to why.

'Andrew, I really think we need to ask about a building on that WhatsApp group. I've been told not to do it but no one has said anything to you, have they?'

And so it was that Andrew put up a simple request asking whether anyone knew of a suitable premises.

Two days later, there was a phone call.

'Andrew, it's Neil. We've met a few times at the pastor's prayer mornings. I remember you praying for me on one occasion. That was really helpful.

'As you know, I help lead the Brethren congregations in Walsall and we've been praying about what to do with one of our buildings. We're merging a couple of congregations and that means that the building in Caldmore will be available from the end of the year. The building is managed by a Christian trust on a tenancy basis, but I'm one of the trustees and I've already spoken to my colleagues.

'The thing is, you won't know this, but a friend and I were praying about the building a couple of months ago, and you came to mind. I felt then that we should offer you the building—and here you are on the WhatsApp group, asking for exactly what we can provide. Can we meet up?'

I wouldn't say Andrew was full-on dancing when he got off the phone, but he was definitely one happy step away from breaking into a full jig! This was to be an amazing gift. Neil explained that he and his wife had been part of that congregation for most of their lives. The previous leader had been his wife's father. There had been a faithful presentation of the gospel in that building for over 100 years. They had observed us on the streets in Walsall and were stirred by what we had been doing, by our boldness and by the results they were witnessing.

We weren't anything like the Brethren in some ways. Ripped jeans and tattoos. Baptised in the Spirit, speaking in tongues. Women leaders. All that the Brethren were definitely not! But God had spoken, and they knew they were to hand over the premises to us.

Their last service in the building was in January 2023. That's when we picked up the keys. That's when God had said we'd have a building. Caldmore Gospel Hall became Keystone Church.

Launch Date

March 2023 saw the formal launch of the church—and the first time we publicly used the new name. Situated next to a number of blocks of flats and a Sikh temple, this was the very area I used to go to as a teenager to smoke cannabis.

As I looked out on that first 'real' congregation, there were many friendly faces—people that had been with us on our journey from the Goth festivals through to the start of the church. Sireon and Ruta were on the front row, having journeyed with us at Charis.

They work with Charis in Scotland today, but they have continued to walk with us on the journey.

Julio and Iris were there too. They never missed a week when we were only able to meet for Bible study, or for walks in Sutton Park. Louise stood at the back—slipping in late, having sorted out the kitchen and drinks for everyone. Louise has only missed one Reboot mission trip so far! Tegan and Andrew stood ready as part of the worship team. Javier had arrived from Spain, also at the back on that first Sunday. In more recent times, we've added Carol, Sharon, Andre and Naomi into our leadership mix.

Throughout our journey, we've been incredibly blessed by the support of Andrew Wommack Ministries and Charis Bible College. While there's no official connection, the friendships we've built through them have been a lifeline—people who've cheered us on, prayed us through, and stood with us in key moments.

At the top of that list are John and Susan Donnelly. I'll never forget walking into the conference that would change everything, and hearing John's voice at the microphone—it was certainly a divine setup! Since then, they've become more than friends. They officiated our wedding, walked with us through the heartbreak of Kaiden's funeral, and continue to mentor and guide us as Andrew and I work out this calling together. Alongside them, I'm grateful for three solid friends—Ali, Lucy and Shirley. We met during my early days at Charis, and they've been the people I turn to when I need practical advice, prayer, or just a bit of straight-talking wisdom. They're steady, reliable and know how to keep things real, which is exactly what I need. Keystone was never meant to be your typical church and it never will be. We don't have a separate outreach department because outreach isn't something we do on the side. It's who we are. Every single one of us.

That said, Keystone isn't Reboot. We don't expect everyone in the congregation to be out on mission trips or in evangelism teams. But the two are deeply connected. This church was born out of Reboot—it grew out of mission—and that DNA will always be part of who we are.

What we never want is to become a 'safe' church. Comfortable. Settled. Instead, we keep asking: What is God calling us to do in Walsall? In this nation? And beyond? We want to stay sharp in our purpose and obedient to the call, wherever it leads.

At the end of the day, Keystone exists because God said so. It was His idea, not ours. We responded in obedience, but it's His church. That's something we have to remember constantly: we're not here to cling to leadership roles, we're here to raise others up. Our heart is to build, disciple and release leaders—not just to lead, but to multiply the mission.

Here's how we think about it: Reboot Ministry is the calling God placed on Andrew and me, personally. Keystone Church is something bigger, it's God's vision for His people in Walsall. It's a subtle distinction, but it keeps us focused and ensures we don't lose our evangelistic edge.

And when we say this church is God's idea, we mean it. We've had people walk through our doors and say things like, 'God told me there was a church somewhere along this road—I just had to find it.' Moments like that remind us that this isn't man-made.

We're still a young church—our average age is around thirty—and we are wonderfully multicultural. People from many nations call Keystone home. The nations are coming to us, even as we go out to the nations. And for that, we are deeply thankful.

Chapter Nineteen

...But Christ Who Lives

Paul writes to the Galatians: 'I have been crucified with Christ. It is no longer I who live, but Christ who lives in me' (Galatians 2:20).

That verse isn't just powerful theology—it's my testimony. It's the truth I live by. My old life? Gone. I don't live for the same things anymore—not for drugs, not for sex, not for unhealthy relationships. Now, it's Christ who lives in me. He's changed everything. I live for Him, and through the Holy Spirit, He lives in me. *It is no longer I who live.*

When I first became a Christian, I was on fire, I still am—eager, grateful and ready to serve in any way I can. Whether it is in church or during my times at Charis Bible College, I just want to be part of what God is doing. I even applied for a job at Charis. It was an admin role. I didn't get it, but something came out of that experience that stayed with me.

During the interview, they asked me, 'If you could do any job, what would it be?' Without thinking twice, I said, 'Missions.'

Missions

Not long after that, a new part-time role opened up: Assistant Missions Coordinator. I applied and got the job. It might not sound like much to some, but for me, it was huge. It was my first real job. Ever.

I'll never forget that first day. Even though I already knew the team from volunteering as a student, this felt completely different. This was official. This was paid. And honestly, I was nervous. Could I do this?

I remember turning to my colleague, Lucy, and asking,

'Lucy, I've been a student here for three years—how am I supposed to act like a staff member?'

She smiled and said something that has stuck with me:

'Selina, you don't have to act like anything. You already are a staff member.'

That role quickly turned into real responsibility. Not long after I started, I was asked to help lead a mission trip to Uganda. It was a big step, and it marked the beginning of something significant in my life. That trip happened near the end of 2019. Then, just a few months later, I led a team to Romania in early 2020.

That Romanian team? We were the last to return before Covid hit and the world shut down.

Zoom in the Car

When lockdown hit, like so many others, I had to adjust. I continued working for Charis, but now from home. As best I could, I carried on teaching first-year students, mostly on 'Spirit, Soul and Body' and 'The Believer's Authority', along with facilitating discussion groups and helping them with their studies. With Andrew at home and four of the kids around, I ended up teaching from our Volkswagen people carrier, parked on the driveway. Not quite the classroom I envisioned!

It was a strange season, but in a way, it gave me space to plan ahead—for what we'd step into once restrictions lifted.

When we returned to college, I was given more responsibility, teaching and coordinating the first-year programme. One of the students that year? My own daughter, Tegan. Teaching your own child comes with a few emotional speedbumps. Yes, there were tears and frustrations. But there were also powerful moments of connection. It was special to see her walking a similar path. She graduated from year two at the Grace and Faith conference, seven years to the day that I got saved at the same conference.

By summer 2021, I was promoted to Missions Coordinator and now had an assistant. I needed God's help more than ever—this was all brand-new territory for me. I'd never had a job before Charis, and suddenly I had someone reporting to *me*. To top it off, I was now one of four on the senior leadership team, overseeing the direction of the college. It was exciting. And a little terrifying.

Fast forward, and I'm now full-time at the college, wearing multiple hats: Missions Supervisor, and Year Two Coordinator. I also teach on evangelism, on flowing in the gifts of the Spirit, as well as on how to pray for people. I oversee fundraising and organise our end of year Graduation Ball.

Beyond my work at the college, I now find myself travelling the world—often leading mission teams, sometimes simply exploring new places for the joy of it. It's almost hard to believe that before becoming a Christian, I had never even set foot on a plane. Since then, I've flown more than fifty times, to Europe, Africa, the USA, South America, the Caribbean and Asia. And Israel—that one will always have a special place in my heart.

Yes, life is busy. But it's also so fulfilling.

The Blue Book

In the middle of all of this, I continued to explore my adoption story. Eventually, the agency handed me a small blue book—a kind of file. Technically, it shouldn't have existed. Mine was meant to be a closed adoption, so everything should have been destroyed. But somehow, it survived.

On the front was my birth name. Inside were records—fragile, emotional pieces of my story. My original birth certificate. Social worker notes about my birth mum, and her struggle over the decision to give me up. She changed her mind—twice. There were details about my time in foster care, and reports assessing whether my adoptive parents were suitable.

It was like opening a time capsule from the earliest part of my life—a part I never got to remember, but now had the chance to understand.

Reading it all, I realised something deeply important: God was always there. The thread of His kindness and mercy was woven through every page. The blue book might document the start of my life, but it doesn't define it. If there were a second book—one I would hold onto more tightly—it would be red, marked by the blood of Jesus, shed for me.

Even in my darkest moments, when I felt most abandoned, I had a Father who saw me. A Saviour who loved me. Who gave His life for me.

He Lives

Today, life is still full-on—but so full of joy. There's nothing like seeing my children walking into the callings that God has for them. Watching someone respond to the gospel out on the streets with Reboot. Seeing people baptised and growing in faith at Keystone. Or watching Charis students graduate, ready to step into ministry with boldness and clarity. It's incredible.

I don't need to look far for evidence that Jesus saves—I see it every day in the mirror. My life is proof. Every person I reach, encourage, teach or love is a testament to the unshakable power of God to transform. Each one reflects the same grace that changed me. My life isn't random. It's evidence of God's faithfulness. A powerful testimony that Jesus saves, restores and makes all things new.

So my prayer for you, as you close this chapter, is simple and bold:

May you also be able to say, with your whole heart, 'It is no longer I who live, but Christ who lives in me.'

Amen.

Endpiece

A Letter from Selina

From My Heart

If you've read this far, you now know my story. You've seen the brokenness I came from, the grace that found me, and the new life Jesus gave me. This book is my testimony, but my prayer is that it's also a spark of hope for you—proof that God can reach anyone, anywhere, and change everything.

If you've read my story and you don't yet know Jesus as your Lord and Saviour, please hear this: He loves you. Right now. Just as you are. You don't have to try harder, earn His love or clean yourself up first. He has already done everything needed to make you right with God—the work was finished on the cross.

The same Jesus who rescued me from addiction, abuse, fear and hopelessness is reaching out to you right now. He knows your pain. He sees every tear. He is ready to forgive you, heal you and give you a brand-new life—a life of peace, purpose and freedom.

If you're ready to take that step, pray these words from your heart:

Lord Jesus, I believe You died for me and rose again. I confess that I need You. Please forgive me for my sins. I surrender my life to You. Come and live in me. Make me new. I choose to follow You from this day forward. Amen.

If you prayed that prayer, you've just stepped into the most important relationship of your life—you are now a child of God. The Bible says all of heaven is rejoicing right now over you!

You are loved. You are seen. And your new life starts today.

Let's Stay Connected

I would love to hear from you—to pray for you, encourage you and help you take your next steps in faith. You don't have to walk this journey alone. In the next section, you'll find my contact details, along with ways you can connect with our ministry, find resources and join a community of believers who will walk alongside you. I look forward to hearing your story and celebrating all that God will do in your life.

Reboot

A Gospel Picture

Imagine this:

God created a virtual world. It was perfect. He loved it deeply and communicated regularly with Adam and Eve—like the way we stay in touch today through texts, DMs, Instagram or messaging apps.

But one day, something changed.

God sent a message... and all He received was a black screen with a flashing red alert: 'ERROR: VIRUS DETECTED.'

The system had been infected.

Sin had entered the world.

Like a virus corrupting everything in its path, sin began to spread—fast. Before long, it had taken control of people's thoughts, decisions and desires. The world was spiralling into chaos: violence, confusion, destruction and death.

But all the while, God was working on the antivirus.

When the time was right, He released it.

The antivirus is Jesus.

When Jesus came to Earth, He made it possible for people to receive the antivirus and install it—to reboot their lives. His life, death and resurrection defeated the power of sin, offering a clean system—a fresh start.

And here's the amazing part: The antivirus doesn't just suppress the virus—it completely removes it.

But that's not where the story ends.

Like any good system, it still needs updates.

If we don't stay connected—if we ignore the updates—we will not get reinfected by sin itself (because Jesus already defeated it), but we will still suffer the effects: anxiety, depression, despair, confusion, brokenness. Our operating system gets clogged. We don't run right.

That's why we need ongoing updates—through prayer, through community, and most importantly, through the Word of God. His Word is our daily download. It strengthens, corrects, renews and restores.

Jesus is the only reboot that brings true life.

The Gospel is not just a one-time install—it's an ongoing transformation.

Will you reboot today?

If this message connected with you, or if you want to reboot your life and receive the antivirus that is Jesus, talk to Him. He's listening. Ask Him to forgive you, to cleanse your heart and to start fresh.

And if you're already a believer—**share this message**. Someone you know might be one prayer away from a brand-new start.

Acknowledgements

First and always, I give thanks to God – Father, Son, and Holy Spirit – for rescuing me, calling me, and giving me this testimony. Without Him, there would be no story to tell.

To my husband, Andrew—thank you for loving me with the love of Christ, for leading beside me in ministry, and for being my safe place in every season. You are living proof of God's power to restore what the enemy tried to destroy.

To my children and grandchildren—you are my joy and my treasure. Thank you for your patience, grace and forgiveness as God has written His redemption into our family story. I am so proud of each of you.

To my parents—thank you for showing me unconditional love and planting seeds of truth that God brought to life in His time.

To my dear friends—you have been constant reminders of His grace and joy in my life. Your love, laughter, and steadfastness have been a gift beyond words.

To Andrew Wommack—thank you for your obedience to the Gospel. Through your ministry I heard the truth, and because of that I was able to step into my God-given destiny.

To Ralph—thank you for helping me to organise my thoughts and bring my story to life on these pages.

To all who helped to produce this book—thank you, Mark Theisinger, for your photography skills; Melanie Milongo and Richard Blaikie for your creativity with the cover concept; Ali Pereira and Nathan Turner for your careful proofreading; and my publisher, Malcolm Down, for your guidance and dedication. Your skill, excellence and faithfulness have helped turn a testimony into a book that I pray will reach countless hearts.

From the bottom of my heart, thank you.

Selina.

Acknowledgements

Selina Brown

Selina Brown is an author, evangelist, international speaker and pastor with a passion for seeing people encounter Jesus, discover their true identity in Him, and walk in lasting freedom. She travels internationally, sharing the Gospel with raw honesty and bold faith, always pointing people directly to Christ.

Selina co-founded Reboot Ministry with her husband, Andrew, and together they pastor Keystone Church in Walsall. She also serves as Year 2 Coordinator and Mission Supervisor at Charis Bible College Walsall, equipping believers to take the Gospel to the nations. She is a proud mother and grandmother, cherishing every moment with her children and grandchildren.

If you would like to **invite Selina to speak** or partner with her ministry in taking the Gospel to the nations, you can connect via email, through her website, via social media or by scanning the QR code provided.

www.selinabrown.org
contact@selinabrown.org

Reboot Ministry—Taking the Gospel to the Broken

Reboot Ministry, co-founded by Selina and Andrew Brown, exists to bring the hope of Jesus into the darkest places—prisons, streets, broken homes and nations in need. Through evangelism, discipleship and international mission trips, lives are being restored by the power of the Gospel. The mission of Reboot Ministry is clear: reach the lost, equip the found and send them into their God-given calling. From the UK to the nations, the team goes where others may not, carrying the message that no one is beyond the reach of God's love.

If you would like to join a mission team, host a team, or support the work of Reboot Ministry, you can connect via email, through their website, via social media or by scanning the QR code provided.

www.rebootministry.org.uk
Andrew.selina@rebootministry.org.uk

Keystone Church Walsall—Where Jesus is the Keystone

At Keystone Church Walsall, lives are being changed through the power of Jesus Christ. Led by pastors Andrew and Selina Brown, this vibrant, Bible-based church in the heart of Walsall is marked by passionate worship, clear biblical teaching and a genuine love for people. It is a place where visitors can encounter Jesus, build real relationships and grow in their faith.

Pastors Andrew and Selina are also available to minister at churches, conferences and evangelistic events both in the UK and internationally. Their ministry is marked by a clear Gospel message, a deep love for people, and a passion to see lives restored and empowered by the Holy Spirit. They are committed to simplifying the Word of God so that everyone can understand it and be transformed.

If you would like to **invite Andrew and Selina to speak,** you can connect via email, through their website, via social media or by scanning the QR code provided.

www.keystonechurch.org.uk
Andrew.selina@keystonechurch.org.uk

Ralph Turner

Ralph Turner is a Christian author specialising in biographies and ghostwritten autobiographies. He has fourteen published books and is based in Leicester, UK.

www.ralphturnerwriter.com